EASTERN FRONT FROM PRIMARY SOURCES

GÖTTERDÄMMERUNG

THE LAST DAYS OF THE WEHRMACHT IN THE EAST

EDITED AND INTRODUCED BY
BOB CARRUTHERS

Pen & Sword
MILITARY

This edition published in 2012 by
Pen & Sword Military
An imprint of
Pen & Sword Books Ltd
47 Church Street
Barnsley
South Yorkshire
S70 2AS

First published in Great Britain in 2012 in digital format by
Coda Books Ltd.

Copyright © Coda Books Ltd, 2012
Published under licence by Pen & Sword Books Ltd.

ISBN 978 1 78159 136 9

A CIP catalogue record for this book is
available from the British Library

Printed and bound by
CPI Group (UK) Ltd, Croydon, CR0 4YY

Pen & Sword Books Ltd incorporates the Imprints of Pen & Sword Aviation, Pen &
Sword Family History, Pen & Sword Maritime, Pen & Sword Military, Pen &
Sword Discovery, Pen & Sword Politics, Pen & Sword Atlas, Pen & Sword
Archaeology, Wharncliffe Local History, Wharncliffe True Crime, Wharncliffe
Transport, Pen & Sword Select, Pen & Sword Military Classics, Leo Cooper, The
Praetorian Press, Claymore Press, Remember When, Seaforth Publishing and
Frontline Publishing

For a complete list of Pen & Sword titles please contact
PEN & SWORD BOOKS LIMITED
47 Church Street, Barnsley, South Yorkshire, S70 2AS, England
E-mail: enquiries@pen-and-sword.co.uk
Website: www.pen-and-sword.co.uk

CONTENTS

INTRODUCTION

THIS BOOK forms part of the series entitled 'Eastern Front from Primary Sources.' The aim is to provide the reader with a varied range of materials drawn from original writings covering the strategic, operational and tactical aspects of the battles of Hitler's war in the east. The concept behind the series is to provide the well-read and knowledgeable reader with an interesting compilation of related primary sources which together build a picture of a particular aspect of the titanic struggle on the Eastern Front.

I am pleased to report that the series has been well received and it is a pleasure to be able to bring original primary sources to the attention of an interested readership. I particularly enjoy discovering new primary sources, and I am pleased to be able to present them unadorned and unvarnished to a sophisticated audience. The sources speak for themselves and the readership I strive to serve is the increasingly well informed community of reader/historians which needs no editorial lead and can draw its own conclusions. I am well aware that our community is constantly striving to discover new nuggets of information, and I trust that with this volume I have managed to stimulate fresh enthusiasm and that some of these articles will provoke readers to research further down these lines of investigation, and perhaps cause established views to be challenged once more. I am aware at all times in compiling these materials that our relentless pursuit of more and better historical information is at the core our common passion. I trust that this selection will contribute to that search and will help all of us to better comprehend and understand the bewildering events of the last century.

The centre piece of this volume is the often overlooked US

An abandoned half-track of the SS Divison 'Nordland' lies forlornly in the ruins of Berlin. The body is that of Swedish volunteer SS-Mann Ragnar Johannson, one of the last men to fall.

Army study 'The German Defense Of Berlin' written by Wilhelm Willemar, Oberst A.D. It is built upon a wide range of primary interviews and carries a foreword by Generaloberst A.D. Franz Halder which is highly illuminating and gives a good insight into the battle for Berlin. This last battle is often presented as an exercise in masterful Teutonic planning. In reality nothing could be further from the truth. The defending force was small (60,000 strong at most) and highly disorganised, which makes it all the more remarkable how such heavy Soviet casualties were incurred in the last few days of the war.

In order to produce an interesting compilation giving a flavour of events at the tactical level I have returned once more to the US Intelligence series of pamphlets, which contain an intriguing series of contemporary articles on weapons and tactics. I find this series of pamphlets particularly fascinating as they are written in the present tense and, as such, provide us with a sense of what was happening at the face of battle as events unfolded. The increasingly desperate battle to stem the flood of Soviet armour is highlighted by the wide range of close combat anti-tank weapons designed to hold back the tanks of the Red Army. The fact that over 2000 Soviet tanks were destroyed in the streets of Berlin is a testament to their effectiveness.

To complete the selection I have drawn upon a small section of the post war debriefs written by General Erhard Raus for the US Army Historical department. Raus is a hugely underrated source and his meetings with Himmler and Hitler are often overlooked. I have included them here as they give an excellent flavour of the frustrations experienced by commanders at the operational level attempting to make things work against a background of constant interference from Hitler.

Thank you very much for buying this volume, I hope you find something new and interesting in these pages and I sincerely hope it earns its place in your library.

Bob Carruthers
Berchtesgaden 2011.

THE GERMAN DEFENSE OF BERLIN

FOREWORD

by Generaloberst a.D. Franz Halder

No cohesive, over-all plan for the defense of Berlin was ever actually prepared. All that existed was the stubborn determination of Hitler to defend the capital of the Reich. Circumstances were such that he gave no thought to defending the city until it was much too late for any kind of advance planning. Thus the city's defense was characterized only by a mass of improvisations. These reveal a state of total confusion in which the pressure of the enemy, the organizational chaos on the German side, and the catastrophic shortage of human and material resources for the defense combined with disastrous effect.

The author describes these conditions in a clear, accurate report which I rate very highly. He goes beyond the more narrow concept of planning and offers the first German account of the

Soviet infantrymen fight their way through the rubble in Berlin.

defense of Berlin to be based upon thorough research. I attach great importance to this study from the standpoint of military history and concur with the military opinions expressed by the author.

LIST OF CONTRIBUTORS

- Colonel Guenther Hartung, Uetzersteig 12 -14, Berlin-Gatow. Colonel Hartung was the leader of a circle of contributors consisting of eight former fellow-combatants living in Berlin. Their contributions have been compiled by him and are included under his name in the supporting studies:
- Lieutenant Colonel Ulrich de Maizieres, Argelander Strasse 105, Bonn, formerly in the Operations Branch of the Army General Staff.
- Colonel Gerhard Roos, Jenaer Strasse 9, Berlin-Wilmersdorf, formerly Chief of Staff of the Inspectorate of Fortifications.
- Colonel Hans-Oscar Woehlermann, Geldernstrasse 48, Koeln-Nippes, formerly Artillery Commander of the LVI Panzer Corps.

In addition to the above-listed home workers, the following persons were included:

- From the Army High Command: Generalmajor Erich Dethlefsen, Generalmajor Illo von Trotha, Colonel Bogislaw von Bonin, Colonel Karl W. Thilo.
- From Army Group Vistula: Generaloberst Gotthard Heinrici, Colonel Eismann.
- From the Replacement Army: Generalmajor Laegeler.
- From Deputy Headquarters, III Corps: Generalleutnant Helmut Friebe, Lieutenant Colonel Mitzkus.
- Commander of the Berlin Defense area, Generalleutnant Helmuth Reymann; his Artillery Commander, Lieutenant Colonel Edgar Platho.

The infamous Katyusha was one of the most feared weapons in the Soviet armoury. These lorry-bourn rocket launchers are being deployed in a Berlin suburb during April 1945.

- From the Wehrmacht Area Headquarters: Major Pritsch, Lieutenant Colonel Karl Stamm.
- From the Luftwaffe: Colonel Gerhardt Trost.
- From Ordnance: Chief Ordnance Technician (Master Sergeant) Schmidt.
- From the Party: Dr. Hans Fritsche.
- Also consulted were the Police Commander for Berlin, Colonel Erich Duensing, and numerous veterans of the fighting, from platoon leaders to regimental commanders, including leaders of such organizations as the Volkssturm and the Plant Protection Service.

1. INTRODUCTION

The research in connection with the present topic proved to be unusually difficult. It becomes evident almost from the start that no long-range, strategic planning for Berlin's defense had ever been conducted. Instead, all plans had been dictated directly by the current situation.

This planning entailed collaboration from the most varied authorities:

(1) Hitler

(2) The Army High Command

(3) The Replacement Army

(4) Army Group Vistula

(5) The Nazi Party, National Defense Commissioner.

Agencies responsible for carrying out the defense plans were:

(1) Deputy Headquarters, III Corps *[Each Wehrkreis, or basic military area, was under the command of a corps headquarters. In wartime this headquarters went into the field and was replaced in the Wehrkreis by a deputy corps headquarters (Stellvertretendes Generalkommando).]*

(2) The Commander of the Berlin Defense Area

(3) Troop units from all branches of the Wehrmacht, the SS, and the Police

(4) the Party Organizations.

Accordingly, the author had to find persons from all of the above organizations who were able to give information. No documents or other written data were discovered, nor was any information found in the later literature of the war which could be considered valid source material.

The only course left to the author was to solicit information from a large number of persons who participated in the

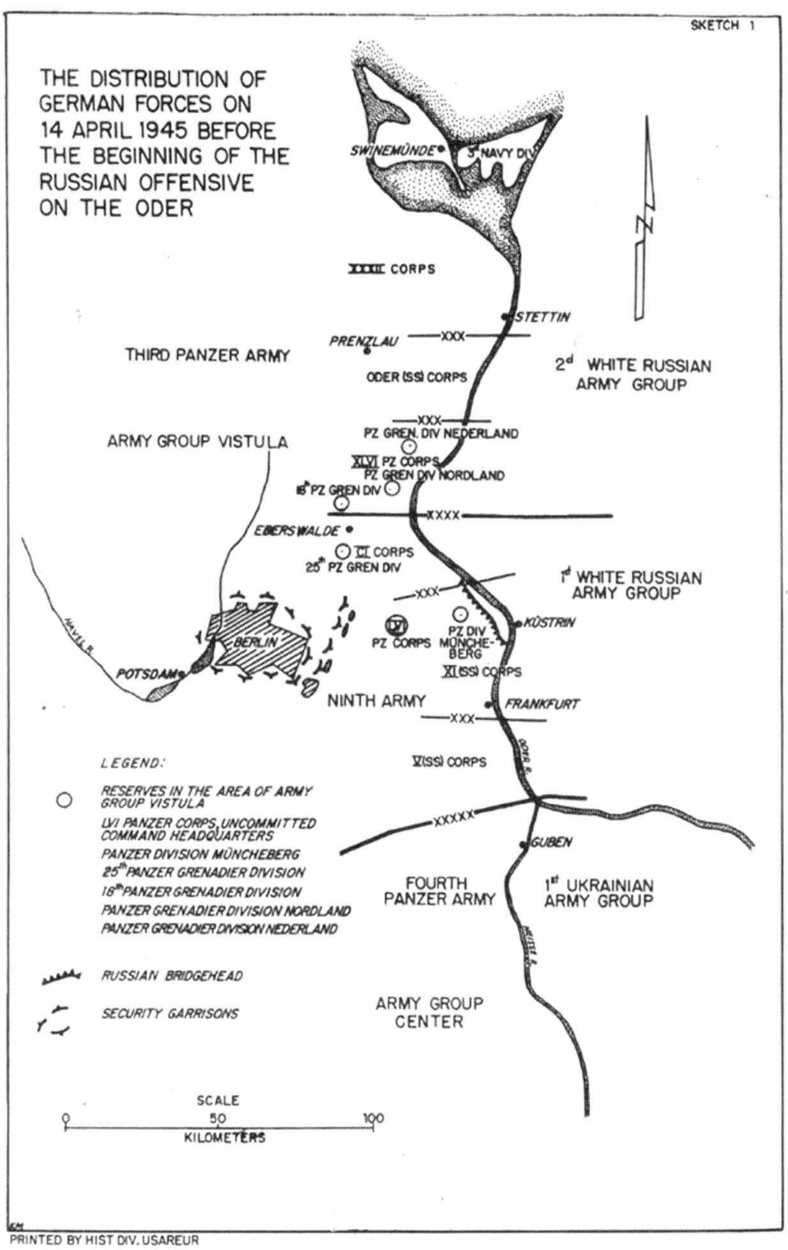

Sketch 1

operation. Nearly all the answers were made from memory, as only a few of the persons questioned are in the possession of notes which they made at the time. Consequently the data thus

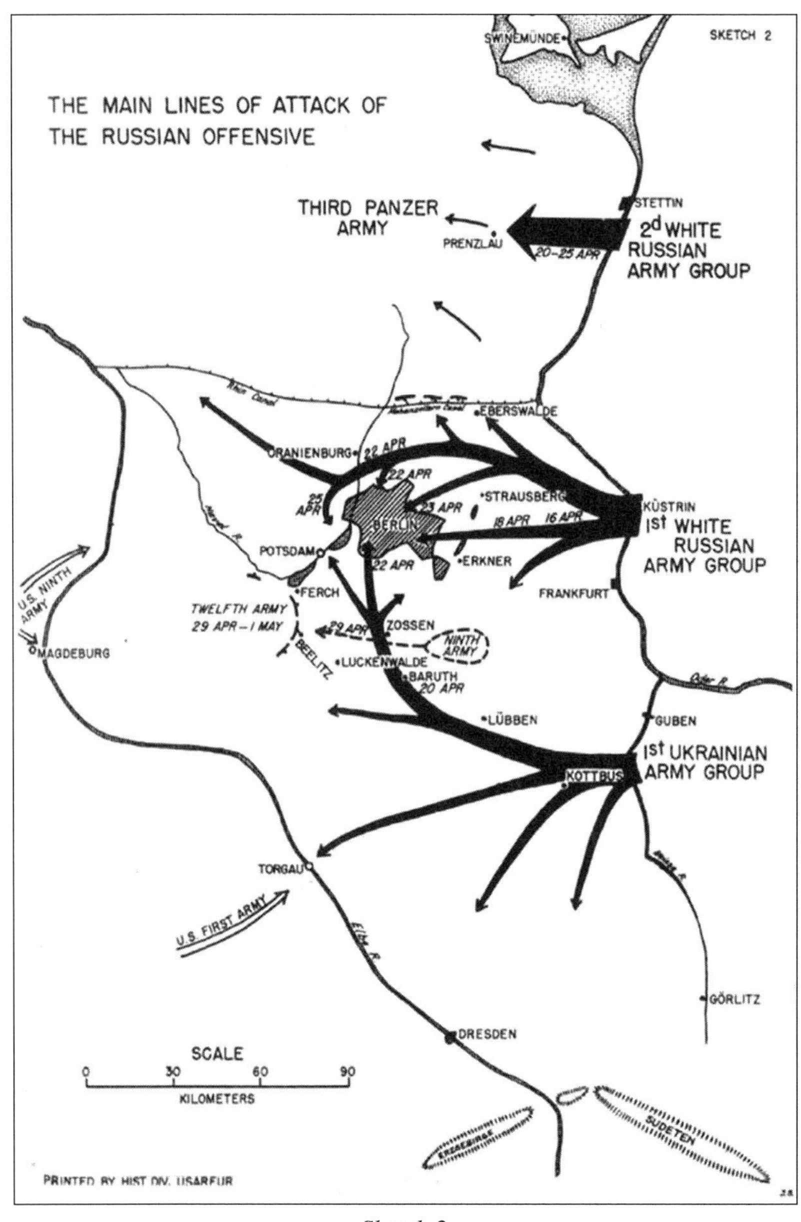

Sketch 2

obtained had to be compared and, where necessary, supplemented and corrected by enlisting the aid of still other collaborators.

Generalleutnant a.D. Reymann, who from 8 March 1945 to

22 April 1945 was Commander of the Berlin Defense Area, for reasons of principle preferred not to collaborate. *[A number of former German officers have refused to collaborate with the Historical Division while their comrades are still imprisoned for war crimes.]* The work, therefore, had to be accomplished without his assistance. Later, at the personal request of the author, General Reymann checked the manuscript for factual accuracy. The drafts were also examined by Generaloberst a.D. Heinrici, former commander of Army Group Vistula. It is assumed, therefore, that an acceptable degree of accuracy was attained. In matters of detail the possibility of error still exists. A few contradictions which could not be fully clarified are indicated in footnotes.

To aid evaluation, this text is accompanied by:

a. A chronological outline of the course of events.

b. Sketch 1, showing the distribution of German forces on 14 April 1945 before the beginning of the large-scale Russian offensive on the Oder.

c. Sketch 2, showing the main lines of attack of the Russian offensive.

In preparing this study, the author acquired an over-all view of the actual course of combat operations. Since it seemed desirable not to overlook the knowledge thus gained a short account of the action is included as an appendix.

Chronological Outline of the Course of Events in the Battle for Berlin

31 January 1945 Weak motorized Russian forces penetrate across the ice of the Oder into the vicinity of Stausberg. Berlin is alerted. February-March The Oder defenses are built up. Early February General der Infanterie von Kortzfleisch, commanding general of Deputy Headquarters, III Corps, and at the same time Commander of the Berlin Defense area, is relieved by Generalleutnant Ritter von Hauenschild.

22 March 1945 Generaloberst Heinrici assumes command of Army Group Vistula.

29 March 1945 Generaloberst Guderian, Chief of the Army General Staff, is relieved by General der Infanterie Krebs.

12-15 April 1945 The Russians make preliminary attacks to widen the Kuestrin bridgehead.

16 April 1945 The Russians begin a large-scale offensive from the Kuestrin bridgehead and across the Neisse.

18 April 1945 Counterattack by the 18th Panzer Grenadier Division is unsuccessful. Oder and Neisse fronts collapse.

19 April 1945 Berlin is placed under the command of Army Group Vistula. The army group assigns SS Obergruppen-fuehrer Steiner the task of safeguarding the Hohen- zollern Canal and vainly requests the withdrawal of the center and right wing of the Ninth Army from the Oder. The Russians push forward from the south to the rear of the Ninth Army in the direction of Berlin.

20 April 1945 The Russians reach Baruth from the south. To the east of Berlin an unsuccessful counterattack is made by the 18th Panzer Grenadier Division and the Panzer Grenadier Divisions "Nordland" and "Nederland." Army Group Vistula orders all available forces to be moved out of Berlin to the defense positions. Hitler decides to remain in Berlin. The Russians launch a large-scale offensive south of Stettin.

21 April 1945 The Soviets reach Zossen, Erkner, and Hopegarten.

22 April 1945 The Russians reach the Teltow Canal near Klein-Machnow from the south and the outskirts of the city at Weissensee and Pankow from the east. They cross the Havel River north of Spandau. Generalleutnant Reymann is replaced by Colonel Kaether. Army Group Vistula is excluded from command in Berlin; the city is placed under Hitler's personal command. Hitler moves Panzer Grenadier Division "Nordland" to Berlin. Army Group Vistula instructs Steiner to launch a relief attack. The LVI Panzer Corps receives orders to proceed to

Weary German infantrymen emerge from a Berlin sub-way station and surrender to the victorious Red Army.

Berlin, but withdraws to the south.

23 April 1945 The Russians attack along the Teltow Canal, against Friedrichshein, and near Tegel. Generalleutnant Weidling becomes Commander of the Defense Area and moves the LVI Panzer Group to Berlin. The Army High Command the Wehrmacht High Command leave Berlin. Hitler orders an attack by the Twelfth Army from the southeast, aiming at Berlin.

24 April 1945 The Russians cross the Teltow Canal; strong fighting progresses in the eastern part of the city. The Russians advance west from Spandau and close off Berlin from the west. Steiner's troops are thrown back to their line of departure after attacking with initial successes.

25 April 1945 The Russians break through south of Stettin.

24 April-1 May1945 Berlin's defenders stage severe retarding actions.

29 April 1945 The Twelfth Army reaches Beelitz-Ferch. General-oberst Heinrici is relieved of the command of Army Group Vistula.

30 April 1945 Hitler commits suicide. Remaining elements of the Ninth Army break through to the Twelfth Army.

1 May 1945 Negotiations for surrender are begun. Elements of the Berlin garrison attempt to escape.

2 May 1945 Berlin surrenders.

2. THE VARIOUS VIEWPOINTS

I. GENERAL

The decision to defend Berlin to the last man was of crucial importance both to the troops involved and, even more, to the city's several million inhabitants. Special attention must be given to the command authorities who made this decision and carried it through and those who attempted to counteract it. Only thus can one see an over-all picture of the plans prepared for the defense of the city.

II. HITLER

To Hitler the defense of every city was important, so that to him it was a foregone conclusion that the capital of the Reich would be defended. Human considerations did not concern him. On the contrary, he stated on numerous occasions that the German people, if defeated, would be unworthy to survive the struggle. The thought of his own downfall cannot have been absent from Hitler's mind during the last months. On the other hand, almost to the very end he seems to have clung - sporadically, at least - to the hope that a shift in front by the Western Allies might change the tide of war. This hope is indicated by repeated statements of the Fuehrer.

Hitler was an advocate of stubborn defense, particularly of cities. The successful defense of Leningrad and Stalingrad by the Russians and of Breslau by the Germans seemed to him to support his views. However, it was no longer possible at this stage of the war for a strategic concept to serve as a basis for the defense of Berlin.

At the beginning of February Hitler declared Berlin a fortified place. By virtue of this proclamation and the fact that all vital

Soviet heavy artillery deployed on the streets of Berlin.

decisions regarding defense measures were made by him personally, he assumed full responsibility in the battle for the capital.

Until the Russians reached the Oder at the end of January 1945, no provisions were made for the defense of Berlin. Certain security measures taken before this time by the Wehrmacht Area Headquarters served only to combat internal disturbances which could be expected from the masses of foreign laborers employed in and around the city.

Hitler now ordered the building up, supplying, and tactical distribution of a security garrison, but failed to set up a general plan of defense stipulating with what forces Berlin was to be defended. The security forces available in the city were far too weak for a protracted defense. Moreover, the best of these troops from the standpoint of combat effectiveness had been moved out of the city to the Oder. Thus the question of forces to be used in the defense depended upon improvisation.

Hitler informed the Commander of the Berlin Defense Area,

Generalleutnant Reymann, that in the event of a battle for the capital sufficient front-line troops would be made available. A plan based on such an "assurance" naturally contained a great element of uncertainty, because it was impossible to know whether troops could be brought in from the eastern front in time and in what condition they would be. No assurance was ever given by Army Group Vistula that such troops could be provided.

At first the defense of Berlin lay along the Oder, and an attempt was made to reinforce that front as much as possible. Upon inquiring at the beginning of April what plan was envisaged in case the Oder front collapsed, Army Group Vistula was told that the Third Panzer Army was to hold fast along the lower Oder, while the army group was to fall back with the Ninth Army to a line along the canals between Eberswald and the mouth of the Havel in order to form a northern Kessel between the lower Elbe and the Oder. *[As used here, Kessel (literally kettle) means an island of defense or an all-round or enclosed defensive area.]* It is not necessary here to discuss the prospects of defending such an extended Kessel. It is important to note, however, that the army group was not ordered to include Berlin in its own defense plan or to divert troops to the city. A large southern Kessel was to be formed concurrently with that in the north. For himself, Hitler foresaw the possibility of retreating to the Bavarian mountain fortress.

Nevertheless, it must not be presumed that, if this plan had been carried out, Berlin would have been abandoned without a struggle. Rather the defense would have been carried out along the pattern established in many other cities by forces ordered up in accordance with the particular circumstances. Meanwhile, in the absence of Hitler, Army Group Vistula and the Commander of the Defense Area would have had greater freedom of operation.

As the collapse of the Oder front became imminent, Hitler tried desperately to close the gaps in the line by giving orders to attack. Even he was forced to admit that the defenders were not succeeding in throwing back the attacking Russian spearheads; nevertheless, it would still have been possible around 19 April to withdraw considerable forces from the Ninth Army into Berlin by abandoning the parts of the Oder front still being held. Hitler, however, bluntly refused Army Group Vistula's urgent daily requests (which were prompted by other considerations) that the Ninth Army be withdrawn from the Oder. Not until 23 and 24 April did he order any troops into Berlin and then only those of the LVI Panzer Corps, which were fighting before the gates of the city. By this time the Russians had already penetrated the city at several points, so that the position along the city perimeter could no longer be occupied according to plan.

As early as 20-22 April Hitler apparently felt that the end was near; in any case, on 20 April he announced his decision to remain in the city. Then, under the influence of his entourage, he gathered courage once more and tried to continue the struggle by defending the capital and at the same time by ordering relief attacks from the west and the north. Here again the hope for a shift in front by the Western Allies may have been a motivating factor. Beginning about 23 April the city put up particularly stiff resistance.

Only after the relief attacks had proven hopeless and a meeting of American and Russian troops had been effected near Torgau without producing the hoped-for clash did Hitler concede defeat and commit suicide. Before his death Hitler issued written orders to the Commander of the Defense Area, leaving him free to attempt a break-out, but forbidding surrender. For a few hours Goebbels, as a minister of the Reich still present in Berlin, stepped into Hitler's place and forbade attempts either to break out or to surrender. He apparently tried at the last moment to come to an agreement with the Russians, offering to surrender on condition that they recognize a new government in which he would take part. When this failed, he also committed suicide.

[Ploetz, Regenten und Regierung der Welt, Teil II (A.G. Ploetz, Verlagsbuchhandlung fuer Aufbau und Wissen, Bielefeld, 1953). Published Allied accounts of the last days in the Reich Chancellory bunker state that Goebbels committed suicide before Hitler.]

Apart from the fact that Hitler's behavior fails to reveal the slightest trace of any feeling of responsibility toward the German people as a physical entity, there are indications that at times his thinking was no longer rational. His estimate of the means at his disposal and the fighting power of the enemy were wholly unrealistic. On the other hand he was by no means insane in the medical sense. To the very end he managed to maintain his authority and power to command. The idea of a revolt in order to surrender the city without a struggle did not even occur to Hitler's immediate associates, since their own destiny was too closely linked to his. Outside this circle revolt was completely out of the question because of the extensive security measures that had been taken and because of the thin dispersal of authority.

Soviet infantrymen dash forward into action during the final assault on Berlin.

III. THE ARMY HIGH COMMAND

The Army High Command had also failed to prepare an advance plan for the defense of Berlin. This may have been largely because those responsible wished to avoid a battle for Berlin. To Hitler's mind it would have been defeatism to take measures for defense west of the Oder as long as the German front was still on the Vistula. Moreover, after the dismissal of Generaloberst Guderian, the Army High Command had been transformed into an agency existing merely to carry out Hitler's orders. The Wehrmacht High Command had already been functioning on this level for a long time.

IV. ARMY GROUP VISTULA

The commander of Army Group Vistula, Generaloberst Heinrici, had developed his own clearly thought-out plan. Assuming that the war would end soon after the anticipated collapse of the Oder front, he was concerned first, with saving as many German soldiers as possible from Russian captivity by shifting his troops to the area overrun by the Western Allies and, secondly, with protecting the population as much as possible from further loss of life and property.

According to this viewpoint a battle for Berlin should be avoided. To this end the army group did everything in its power.

At first Army Group Vistula agreed with Hitler that all available forces should be committed on the Oder front. In the plan for a northern and a southern Kessel the army group saw the possibility of moving the Ninth Army on either side of Berlin and past the city to the northwest. This was emphatically recommended to Ninth Army. In accordance with this recommendation the army's service trains not needed in the fighting were actually diverted toward the Mecklenburg area.

Undoubtedly the implementation of this plan would have been difficult for the combat elements of the Ninth Army, for the attack of the Russians was expected precisely along its left wing,

T-34 tanks in the inner city streets of Berlin.

which was the pivot point of any withdrawal to the northwest. The army group made allowance for this in advance by distributing its mobile reserves behind the left wing of Ninth Army, even going so far as to echelon them rearward a little toward the left. (See Sketch 1 on page 11)

If the center and right wing of this army had been pulled back in time and full use had been made of the defense position for a delaying action, it would certainly have been possible to save the bulk of the Ninth Army and to preserve the coherence of the army group.

As the Russian break-through to Berlin took shape, Army Group Vistula ordered the Commander of the Defense Area, Generaloberst Reymann, to move all available troops still fit for immediate action out of Berlin and into the defense position east of the city. These troops would then not be available for the actual battle for Berlin. A penetration of the defense positions would have resulted in the occupation of the city without a struggle, and the population would have been spared the horrors of a battle. The army group estimated that the first Russian armored units would reach the Reich Chancellory as early as 22

'Desyanti'- Soviet tank riders on their way into the battle for Berlin.

April. However, the measure ordered by the army group was only partially carried out. Only some thirty battalions were put on the march, General Reymann explaining that the limitation had been imposed by lack of transport facilities and the poor condition of the remaining battalions. Thus the bulk or the security forces stayed in Berlin.

The army group's intention not to let any parts or the Ninth Army reach Berlin was also frustrated. Without consulting either the army group or Ninth Army or even informing them beforehand, Hitler withdrew the LVI Panzer Corps into Berlin. Requests by army group that the bulk of Ninth Army be saved from encirclement on the central Oder and withdrawn to the south of Berlin were refused. On the contrary, orders emanating directly from the Fuehrer instructed the Ninth Army in the sharpest terms to hold fast along the Oder.

For its part, on 22 April Ninth Army had ordered the LVI Panzer Corps to attempt a junction with the army southeast of Berlin. At the same time the commanding general of this corps,

General der Artillerie Weidling, received Hitler's first order to move into Berlin. General Weidling decided not to go to Berlin, but to try to make contact with the Ninth Army to the south. Only after the order had been repeated on 23 April did he move the corps to Berlin.

After the encirclement had been completed, Hitler ordered relief attacks aimed at Berlin. These were to be carried out by the Ninth Army from the south, the Twelfth Army from the west, and Army Group Vistula from the north. Army Group Vistula was to send all available forces to SS Obergruppenfuehrer Steiner in the area west of Oranienburg for an attack on Berlin-Spandau. Here too there arose a fundamental difference of opinion between Hitler and the army group.

Generaloberst Heinrici maintained that the ordered attack had absolutely no prospect of success. Consequently, in estimating the situation, he felt that bringing together all available forces near Oranienburg, as instructed, would necessarily lead to the destruction of the Third Panzer Army and Group Steiner as well, since the lines of the Third Panzer Army already had been pierced south of Stettin by strong Russian armored forces. In his opinion the formation of a group near Oranienburg was tactically desirable; not, however, to attack Berlin, but to protect the deep flank of the Third Panzer Army. All remaining available troops, however, had to be either sent to the Third Panzer Army, in order to make possible its withdrawal to the west (about 250 kilometers on foot), or used to extend the flank protection from Oranienburg to the junction of the Havel and Elbe Rivers, since a Russian thrust to the rear of the army group in the direction of Hamburg was taking shape in that sector.

The divergence in points of view led to a sharp clash between the army group and General Keitel, who urged holding the eastern front of the army group and attacking near Oranienburg. General Keitel relieved General Heinrici of his command on 29 April. The withdrawals to the west were already well under way,

A Soviet rifleman peers carefully round the corner of a bridge in an attempt to locate a German sniper.

however, so that it was still possible under General Heinrici's successor to "save" the bulk of the forces by letting them be captured by the Western allies.

V. SUMMARY

This examination of the various viewpoints shows that Hitler and the Army High Command did not have a unified, constructive plan for the defense of Berlin, but that, apart from preparations for consolidating the limited resources at hand, the conduct of the defense was dependent at any given time on the situation as dictated by the Russians.

General Heinrici's viewpoint could not prevail, since he did not have command authority at the decisive time and place. More will be said of this in the next chapter.

3. ORGANIZATIONAL PLANNING

I. GENERAL

It is a matter of general knowledge that the German conduct of the war was characterized by top level disorganization, which increased as the war progressed.

The various theaters of war, were divided between the Wehrmacht High Command and the Army High Command. Even after the eastern and western front had begun to draw closer together, a co-ordinated plan for the conduct of the war was not forthcoming. The Chief of the Army General Staff through the Operations Branch was responsible for operations only on the eastern front, whereas, the other branches also under the Army General Staff - such as the Organization, Transportation, Signal, and Supply and Administration Branches - were responsible for their respective services on all fronts.

Hitler seriously interfered with Army command channels by issuing direct orders. On the other hand, there was no clear and definite procedure for co-operation between the various branches of the Wehrmacht. The Luftwaffe, Navy, and Waffen-SS each operated on a highly independent basis to the detriment of the armed forces as a whole. The Todt Organization, and to a lesser degree the Reich Labor Service, followed military directives only within limits. The lack of co-ordination and the antagonism between the Wehrmacht and the Party led to strong tensions.

The cause of this confusion in the distribution of authority, which was an expression of profound spiritual disorganization, lay above all in Hitler's deep-rooted mistrust of his generals and the General Staff. By dividing authority, he tried to keep all the reins of command in his own hand.

One of the last defenders of Berlin lies lifeless before the Brandenberg gates.

These circumstances were bound to have a fatal effect on the defense plans and on the battle for the capital, the seat of all top-level agencies of the Reich. It is a basic military principle that under such conditions all command authority should be concentrated in the hands of the commander responsible for the defense. In Berlin, however, this principle was disregarded to an even greater extent than in Breslau or Koenigsberg.

II. MILITARY AGENCIES TAKING PART IN THE DEFENSE

Until 1 February 1945 the military needs of Berlin were the responsibility of the Wehrmacht Area Headquarters. This headquarters was subordinate to Deputy Headquarters, III Corps, and the latter, in turn, to the Replacement Army. The Replacement Army was directly subordinate not to the Army High Command but to the Wehrmacht High Command. The commander of the Replacement Army was the Reichsfuehrer of the SS, Heinrich Himmler.

When at the beginning of February - probably on 1 February 1945 - Berlin was declared a fortified place, Deputy Headquarters, III Corps, while still retaining the functions previously assigned to it, was designated the office of "Commander of the Berlin Defense Area." Initially, the commander was General der Infanterie von Kortzfleisch; as of the beginning of February, he was replaced by Generalleutnant Ritter von Hauenschild.

Under the latter's successor, Generalleutnant Reymann, the office of "Commander of the Berlin Defense Area" was separated from Deputy Headquarters, III Corps.

On 19 April the Commander of the Berlin Defense Area was subordinated to Army Group Vistula. *[General Reymann, Colonel Eismann, and Generaloberst Heinrici give conflicting information regarding the date of this change. The date indicated here, given by Heinrici, is the most probable since it is based on diary entries.]*

On 22 April this order was revoked, and Berlin was placed directly under the Army High Command. On the same day General Reymann was relieved of his post as Commander of the Defense Area and assigned as commander of Armeegruppe Spree. *[An Armeegruppe is a weak improvised Army under an army commander with an improvised army staff.]* Colonel Kaether succeeded him as Commander of the Defense Area.

On 23 April the commanding general of the LVI Panzer Corps, General der Artillerie Weidling, became Commander of the Berlin Defense Area, while still retaining command of his corps.

On 23 - 24 April the Army High Command and Wehrmacht High Command left Berlin; on 25 April these agencies were merged.

III. AUTHORITY OF THE INDIVIDUAL MILITARY AGENCIES

l. Wehrmacht Area Headquarters.

The Wehrmacht Area Headquarters was under Deputy Headquarters, III Corps, and consequently under the Replacement Army. Its tasks included the usual administrative and housekeeping duties of a garrison headquarters, as well as the guarding of bridges, supply depots, and foreign workers, a great number of whom were in Berlin. It also collaborated in removing debris caused by bombing and especially in clearing thoroughfares.

For this purpose the Wehrmacht Area Headquarters had at its disposal military police, guard battalions (local security units), a few construction battalions, and the Berlin Guard Regiment. When Berlin was declared a fortified place, however, it was not the Wehrmacht Area Headquarters that was charged with the defense, but Deputy Headquarters, III Corps, which was designated as the office of the "Commander of the Greater Berlin Defense Area."

The Wehrmacht Area Headquarters retained its earlier functions, with emphasis placed on rounding up the numerous stragglers. Its participation in the defense was consequently of a secondary nature, especially since, with the beginning of the battle, the task of rounding up stragglers was largely taken over by the Party Security Service.

2. Deputy Headquarters, III Corps (Simultaneously Office of the Commander of the Berlin Defense Area).

In addition to its function as Deputy Headquarters, this agency was responsible for the defense of the Wehrkreis and of the Berlin Defense Area.

A T-34 in the thick of the last battles for Berlin.

Accordingly, after the collapse of the Vistula front, the commanding general - initially General der Infanterie von Kortzfleisch - organized a rear defense position east of the Oder and, when this was immediately pierced, another position on the Oder itself. In the midst of this undertaking, at the beginning of February 1945, General von Kortzfleisch was removed from his post. The reason for this action is to be sought in the poor relations which had developed between him and the Gauleiter *[Official in charge of a Nazi Party administrative area]* for Berlin, Goebbels, whose encroachments on the authority of the Army General von Kortzfliesch had sharply opposed.

Generalleutnant Ritter von Hauenschild was appointed his successor, and was relieved of responsibility for the Oder front by Army Group Vistula. Under his command the preparations for the defense of Berlin were begun.

To have one person performing a dual mission proved to be a disadvantage, however. As commanding general of the Deputy Headquarters and commander of Wehrkreis III, General von

Hauenschild's primary task was to send as many troops as possible to the Oder front. As Commander of the Berlin Defense Area, it was in his interest to retain as many troops as possible in Berlin. As a result, the defense of Berlin received secondary consideration.

When General von Hauenschild became sick at the beginning of March 1945, Generalleutnant Reymann was appointed his successor. The new commander separated the Defense Area and the Deputy Headquarters. He himself became Commander of the Defense Area, while General der Pioniere Kuntze was named Deputy Headquarters Commander. The Deputy Headquarters was thereby excluded from command in the defense of Berlin. The headquarters staff left the city shortly before the encirclement.

3. Commander of the Defense Area (After Separation from Deputy Headquarters, III Corps).

Generalleutnant Reymann was assigned his own staff. His Chief of Staff was Colonel (GSC) Refior. Under Generalleutnant Reymann all preparations for the defense were energetically continued, even though, because of limited means, only makeshift measures could be taken.

The Defense Area was divided into eight sectors, designated by the letters A through H. These sectors radiated outward from the position along the town circuit railroad. In each sector a field grade or general officer was assigned as sector commander with the authority of a division commander. For this it was necessary to fall back on officers from antiaircraft artillery and home army units who lacked practical combat experience. Even in filling sub-sector command positions, persons with front-line experience were rarely available.

On 23 April 1945, just as the Russians were at the very gates of the city, Generalleutnant Reymann was relieved of his post and appointed commander of Armeegruppe Spree, which for practical purposes consisted of one under strength division. His removal from Berlin was obviously ordered at the insistence of Goebbels whose initially favorable attitude toward General Reymann had radically altered. When Generaloberst Heinrici, to whom Berlin was at this time subordinate, learned of the change, he ordered General Reymann to remain at his post because it seemed to him foolhardy to change commanders at a time when the danger was most acute. He was not able to make his orders prevail, however, and General Reymann was forced to take over command of Armeegruppe Spree. With part of this force he was driven back to Potsdam and surrounded.

Meanwhile, on 22 April, a new commander was sought. General Kuntze was named first, but for reasons of health he declined. Next a major was considered for the appointment, but was rejected as too young. Finally, Colonel Kaether, until then leader of the National-Socialist guidance officers, became Commander of the Defense Area. For this purpose he was promoted first to Generalmajor and immediately afterward to Generalleutnant, in both cases, however, only for the duration of this appointment. This was a unique occurrence in the German Army; but the promotions were of little use to Kaether, as he was in command for barely two days.

On the evening of 23 April Hitler ordered the commanding general of the LVI Panzer Corps, General der Artillerie Weidling, under the threat of death, to report to the Fuehrer Bunker. It was generally supposed that General Weidling would be shot because his troops had been thrown back by the Russians. Weidling, however, made such a favorable impression that Hitler immediately appointed him Commander of the Defense Area while retaining him as commander of the panzer corps. Thus he became the fifth commander of the Defense Area in less than three months and the third within two days.

General Weidling utilized parts of the Reymann staff, so that in addition to his chief of staff, Colonel (GSC) Von Duffing, Colonel (GSC) Refior was retained as deputy chief of staff. His artillery commander, Colonel Woehlermann, assumed command of all artillery in Berlin; Lieutenant Colonel Platho, who until then had been artillery commander of the Defense Area, was subordinated to him.

General Weidling placed two sectors of the Defense Area under each of his four division commanders in order to integrate the permanent local organization with leadership possessing front-line experience. In carrying out this plan, he immediately encountered opposition. One valiant but self-willed sector commander, Lieutenant Colonel Baerenfaenger, who had just been promoted to Generalmajor, refused to become subordinate to the front-line division commander responsible for his sector. Such difficulties coupled with the necessity for immediately employing the incoming troop units of the panzer corps at the focal points of the battle resulted in constant changes and delays, so that it can hardly be said that the planned organization actually became operative.

The command post of the Defense Area was at first located in a building of the corps headquarters on Hohenzollerndamm. As the Russians approached this vicinity on 25 April it was moved to the Bendler Bunker. General Weidling himself found it necessary to remain most of the time at the Reich Chancellory.

4. Army Group Vistula.

Berlin lay only seventy kilometers to the rear of the main line of resistance of the army group, whose position extended from the junction of the Neisse and Oder Rivers to the Baltic and whose front lines roughly followed the course of the Oder.

In case of a Russian breakthrough, Berlin was to have been incorporated immediately into the army group's zone of operations. The protection of the Reich capital necessarily lay in the latter's hands.

It would therefore have been logical to place the Defense Area under the army group from the start. While this was not done, the army group had expected that such a subordination of

The Zoo Flaktower represented a small fortress which held out against Soviet armoured attacks. The wrecked Russian tanks provide mute proof of the severity of the fighting.

command would be effected at the critical moment and had asked to be informed by General Reymann or his chief of staff of the progress of all defensive measures. The army group also tried to prevent the demolitions from being carried out, in order to save the civilian population from their far-reaching consequences. General Heinrici reserved to himself the decision to order the demolitions in case the Defense Area should be subordinated to his command.

On 19 April, after the collapse of the Oder front east of Berlin, the Defense Area was placed under the command of the army group. Therefore the latter proceeded to carry out its plan for moving all battle-worthy security troops out of Berlin and into the defense position. This intention was only partially realized.

Since the army group could scarcely handle the mass of requests and decisions relative to Berlin from its headquarters near Prenzlau, it in turn placed the Defense Area under Ninth

Army, which was fighting east of the city. However, the army commander, General der Infanterie Busse, refused to accept this responsibility on the valid grounds that in the thick of battle he could not concern himself with the Defense Area, especially since the Ninth Army's center and right wing were still fighting on the Oder. The army group thereupon rescinded the order and retained direct command of Berlin.

The difficult question of the chain of command might conceivably have been solved by introducing a new army command (possibly under SS Obergruppenfuehrer Steiner) between the Ninth Army and the Third Panzer Army with headquarters in Berlin. Under this command could have been placed the Defense Area and all forces south of Berlin (Armeegruppe Spree), east of Berlin (the forces guarding the forward defense position and the LVI Panzer Corps), and northeast of Berlin (security detachments in the Eberswalde - Oranienburg area). This solution would not only have required preparation, however, but it ran counter to the plan of the army group to evacuate the city without fighting.

The subordination of the Defense Area to Army Group Vistula ended when Hitler assumed direct command of Berlin on 22 April.

Even during the time that the army group commanded the Defense Area, Hitler interfered with the chain of command. This is especially evident in the dismissal of General Reymann without consultation with the army group and over its protests. Armeegruppe Spree which was to counter the Russian thrust from the south by way of Luebbenau, was subordinated neither to Army Group Vistula, Ninth Army, nor the Defense Area, but was placed directly under the Army High Command.

A particularly flagrant interference with the command authority of the army group occurred on 23 April when Hitler moved the LVI Panzer Corps, which was subordinate to Ninth Army, into Berlin without informing either the army or the army

This King Tiger was one of the last Panzers to engage in battle. These machines were impervious to many Soviet weapons and were more often destroyed by their crews who ran out of ammunition or fuel.

group. This action had the following consequences:

a. Berlin obtained troops which for a while were able to carry on the battle for the city.

b. The Ninth Army was now outflanked from the north as well as from the south and thereby encircled.

c. Army Group Vistula disintegrated and the Russians were able to push westward, north of Berlin.

Within the LVI Panzer Corps difficulties of command also arose. SS Panzer Grenadier Division "Nordland" tried to break away from the LVI Panzer Corps, to which it was subordinate, and effect a junction with the security troops of SS Obergruppenfuehrer Steiner. This intention was not carried out, since on direct orders from Hitler, and again without corps' knowledge, the division was brought straight to Berlin. This incident led to the temporary dismissal of the division commander.

5. The Army High Command.

A clear decision to determine who would command the Defense Area had not been made by the Army High Command. From the beginning Berlin should have been placed either under Army Group Vistula or the Army High Command. Instead, orders came exclusively in the form of instructions from the Fuehrer. The commander of the Defense Area was left "hanging in the air," since he could not consult Hitler on every detail.

The subordination of the Defense Area to Army Group Vistula would have clarified the situation if Hitler and the Army High Command had not constantly issued orders outside of command channels. Once the army group was excluded from command, however, complete subordination of the Defense Area to Hitler became clearly established. Hitler was now nominal as well as actual combat commander of Berlin.

With the exception of certain individuals, the Army High Command and the Wehrmacht High Command left Berlin on 23 - 24 April. On 25 April the two agencies were merged. On Hitler's behalf, Field Marshall Keitel and Generaloberst Jodl now urged the Twelfth Army and Army Group Vistula to launch relief attacks. The contradictory views which now came to light led on 29 April to General Heinrici's removal, a move, however, which could no longer affect the fate of Berlin.

IV. CIVIL AGENCIES

1. Reich Defense Commissioner.

Along with the military agencies, the Gauleiters, as Reich Defense Commissioners were responsible for the defense of the Reich territory. They were responsible for all measures regarding the civilian population, the organization and training of the Volkssturm, and the construction of field fortifications.

There was no clearly-defined division of authority between the military agencies and the Reich Defense Commissioners, although they were expected to work together. The territorial authority of the Army ended ten kilometers behind the battle line. To the rear of this line, all measures of a purely military nature - even the construction of field fortifications by civilian labor -

were subject to the approval of the Reich Defense Commissioner. He was also responsible for carrying out these measures with the aid of the civilian population and the Volkssturm.

This dualism had serious consequences. In many instances, especially in the construction of field fortifications, the Army attempted to take matters into its own hands, while the Reich Defense Commissioners jealously guarded their own prerogatives. The atmosphere between the two authorities tended to be highly strained.

As a result, numerous rear positions were laid out without the slightest understanding of tactical requirements. A great number of antitank obstacles were constructed, which were either totally ineffective or so hindered friendly troop movements that they had to be destroyed. Construction workers and materials were taken away from the forces in the field. Weapons and ammunition urgently needed to arm strong young replacement troops were hoarded for use by old Volkssturm men far to the rear.

The Volkssturm, the tactical use of which was to have been left to the discretion of military authorities, received orders from the Party even during battle. One report describes how during the fighting a Volkssturm battalion in Berlin received orders alternately from both the sector commander and the Party district headquarters. Since these orders were usually contradictory, the battalion commander was genuinely happy when the Party district headquarters was destroyed by bombs.

The Reich Commissioner for Berlin, Goebbels, and the Commissioner for Brandenburg, Stuerz, often worked at cross purposes. In one instance, without telling anyone, Stuerz withdrew a Brandenburg Volkssturm battalion that was assigned in Berlin, leaving a gap in the city's defense lines on the following day.

Goebbels clearly regarded the Commander of the Defense

Area as his subordinate. Talks between the two took place in Goebbels' office. Every Monday a so-called "major meeting of the War Council" took place under Goebbels' leadership to discuss the defense. Those taking part included the combat commanders, representatives of the Luftwaffe and the Labor Service, the Mayor of Berlin, the Chief of Police, the Commander of the Wehrmacht Area Headquarters, the Administrative District Chief, higher-ranking SS and police leaders, SA Standartenfuehrer Bock, and representatives of the Berlin industries. Goebbels also issued "orders for the defense" which prescribed certain military measures. His influence on the dismissal of commanders has already been shown.

In describing the harmful influence of the Reich Defense Commissioner, it must not be overlooked that the rigorous utilization of the civilian population provided the troops in the field with additional forces, particularly construction manpower. Natlonal-Socialist terror tactics, combined with clever propaganda, made unlikely any attempts on the part of some of the population to sabotage the combat effort of the field troops.

2. The Hitler Youth.

The Hitler Youth were led by Reich Youth Leader Axmann, who called them up for battle and committed them to action, partly on his own initiative and partly in agreement with the Commander of the Defense Area. On 24 April a Hitler Youth brigade armed with Panzerfaeuste *[a recoilless antitank grenade and launcher, both expendable. The German plural of Panzerfaust is Panzerfaeuste.]* appeared in the Strausberg region to hunt down Russian tanks on a freelance basis. In response to urgent protests from General Weidling, Axmann tried to withdraw this youthful and inexperienced brigade from the fighting, but he was no longer able to get his orders through.

In Berlin itself the Hitler Youth fought partly in separate battalions and partly as small units attached to the field forces or the Volkssturm.

This use of the Hitler Youth as a combat force had not been anticipated, and their commitment was not included in the plans of the Defense Area. When eventually called upon, the Reich Youth Leader and subordinate Hitler Youth leaders loyally followed instructions of the military agencies.

3. Other Agencies.

The Reichsfuehrer of the Waffen-SS and Reichsmarschall Goering refrained from exerting direct influence on the issuing of orders. Both, however, held back appreciably strong forces in the vicinity of Berlin as a personal bodyguard, and released these troops only hesitatingly and tardily. Consequently, they could not be included in the defense plans. All attempts by Army Group Vistula to secure blanket authority over these troops were unsuccessful.

The lst Flak Division, which was assigned to Berlin, did not become subordinate to the Defense Area until initial contact had been made with the enemy. The difficulties of planning inherent in this arrangement were reduced by collaboration with the division commander, Generalmajor Sydrow.

On the other hand, little co-operation was received from SS Brigadefuehrer Mohnke, commander of the SS troops responsible for the security of the government quarter. Only with the beginning of the fighting were these troops subordinated to the Defense Area.

The Todt Organization, and to a lesser extent the Reich Labor Service, in many instances evaded orders to the Commander of the Defense Area by invoking their own authority.

V. THE COMMAND SYSTEM

The giving of commands and the transmission of messages suffered from the fact that the command system was no longer equal in all sectors to the demands of a major battle. Not only minor units, but whole divisions, as well as the headquarters of CI Corps, the staff of Army Group Vistula, and the staffs of the

Berlin defense sectors, were improvised in the greatest haste.

There were serious shortages of trained signal personnel, signal equipment, motor vehicles, and gasoline. The lack of telephone equipment could partly be compensated for, since fighting on home territory made possible full use of the peacetime telephone network. This advantage was outweighed, however, by the fact that newly-created task forces and staffs could not acquire any experience in working together. As a result, there was insufficient information at higher levels regarding the actual situation on vital sectors of the front, and communication through command channels was often slow.

Thus, from 18 April on, the Ninth Army and Army Group Vistula were inadequately informed as to the situation on the Ninth Army's northern wing. Army Group Vistula knew nothing about the appearance of Russian tanks south of Berlin near Baruth on 20 April. The permanent local units along the Teltow Canal were completely surprised to find themselves face to face with Russian tanks on 22 April. The bringing up of Panzer reserves (Panzer Grenadier Divisions "Nordland" and "Nederland") to the breach in the Oder defense line took an unduly long time.

VI. SUMMARY

A well-conceived and energetic plan for instituting defense measures and conducting the battle could have been realized only if the responsible commander of the Defense Area had received uniform instructions and been given over-all authority at lower levels. Instead, he was subject to orders and instructions from both military and civil authorities, whose varied interests were apt to be conflicting or inconsistent. This may be illustrated further by the following incident.

General Reymann intended to convert the main east-west thoroughfare of the city *[Charlottenburgerstrasse]* into an airplane landing strip. For this purpose it was necessary to

Soviet heavy armour in the streets of Berlin.

remove the bronze lamps along the street and the nearby trees in the Tiergarten, which had already been severely torn up by bombs.

To do this General Reymann had to obtain Hitler's personal authorization. Hitler gave permission to remove the street lamps, but not the trees. As the dismantling of the street lamps got under way, Reich Minister Speer, who was charged with plans for rebuilding Berlin, raised objections and obtained from Hitler an order forbidding their removal. General Reymann was forced to call on Hitler again in order to procure another authorization to proceed.

While relations between the commander and the agencies above him were badly strained, the distribution of authority at lower levels was even more chaotic. The commander in Berlin had unlimited authority only over the few Army units present in the city. He had only very limited authority over the Volkssturm, (the bulk of the available defense forces), SS troops, Flak units, Hitler Youth, and the Todt Organization and Labor Service. He had no authority at all over the population, which carried the

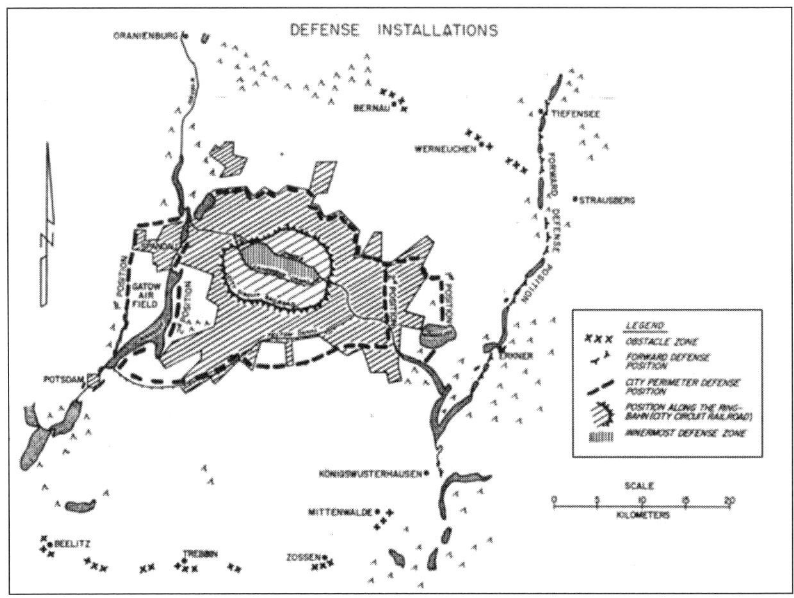

Sketch 3 Defense Installations

greatest burden in the construction of positions.

Another example will serve to illustrate this limitation of authority. The Commander of a battery manned by permanent local troops received a Volkssturm platoon to serve his guns. Yet, he was not allowed to give these men orders except during battle, and so was reduced to using persuasion.

Under these circumstances even a man with the clear vision and conscious purpose of Generalleutnant Reymann could accomplish little.

The broad organizational picture gives indications of complete chaos. The overlapping, confusion, and contradiction in the issuing of orders, the precipitous changes in the distribution of authority, and the constant dismissal and elimination of responsible individuals are signs of fundamental disintegration and imminent collapse. The effects on the fighting troops were devastating. Even now all accounts by veterans of the fighting in Berlin speak of a complete breakdown in leadership, and many even of sabotage. This impression was certain to be widespread.

Just what happened to a commander who failed to defend a fortified place to the last man can be seen in the case of the Commander of Koenigsberg, General der Infanterie Lasch. General Lasch was sentenced in absentia to death by hanging; the sentence was made public in a communique of the High Command and his whole family was placed under arrest.

The object of this study is neither to accuse nor to justify. Nevertheless, the conclusion must be reached that it was not incompetence - apart from individual instances - nor sabotage that led to the downfall of Berlin, but the disorganization of the command system, brought about by Hitler. Neither resigned obedience nor attempts by individuals to act responsibly and intelligently on their own initiative could have availed.

4. THE DEFENSE POSITIONS

I. GENERAL

1. The Geographical Situation.

The only major natural barriers which effectively protect the city of Berlin are the Havel lakes to the west and the Dahme River and the Mueggelsee to the southeast. Because of their narrow width the Teltow Canal to the south and the Spree River and the Landwehr Canal in the heart of the city are only minor obstacles. Protection against tanks is offered by the canals and irrigated fields which lie to the northeast of the city. Thus in the south and north and along most of its eastern flank the city is almost completely open to attack.

Extending around Berlin at a distance of 30-50 kilometers to the south, east, and north is a wooded area in which lakes, rivers, and canals constitute impediments to advancing troops. Of particular importance is the belt of woods and lakes to the east which runs past Koenigswusterhausen, Erkner, and Tiefensee toward the old Oder River near Bad Freienwalde.

A close-knit network of roads surrounds Berlin. The open terrain consists mostly of sandy, easily passable ground. A covered approach to the outskirts of the city is facilitated by patches of woods to the southeast and northeast and in most other places by extensive parks.

Within the city limits the burned-out ruins and fields of debris resulting from bombing raids favored defensive action.

2. Tactical Considerations.

At first Berlin was to be defended at the Oder. Because all troops were needed there, no thought was given to plans for a protracted defense in the wooded area mentioned above. Such a position would have extended over more than 200 kilometers. Nevertheless, the belt of woods and lakes from Erkner to Tiefensee was prepared as a position for defense against an attack from the east.

At a distance or about thirty kilometers beyond the city perimeter an "obstacle ring" was to delay the enemy's approach. All larger localities between the obstacle ring and the city perimeter were to become tactical strong points.

The actual defense was to be carried out along the perimeter itself, full use being made of available obstacles. Even this position extended along a circumference of about one hundred kilometers. At least one hundred battle-worthy divisions would normally have been required to occupy it, whereas the Commander of the Defense Area had at his disposal as infantry only 60,000 Volkssturm troops, one-third of whom were unarmed and two-thirds poorly armed. In addition there were between twenty and thirty artillery batteries and the city's permanent antiaircraft units.

Since Berlin was to be defended to the last house even after the loss or the perimeter position, it was also necessary to make defense preparations in the heart of the city. The city circuit railroad, which extended over a distance of thirty-five kilometers, offered a coherent line for this purpose. Still farther towards the city center, the island formed by the Landwehr Canal and the Spree River was foreseen as a defense position. If the enemy penetrated even here, then individual buildings, such as the Reichs Chancellery, the Reichstag Building, the Bendler Block, and the air raid shelters, were to be defended.

3. Manpower and Means Available for Construction.
Engineer forces subordinate to the Commander of the Defense Area were commanded by Colonel Lobeck. Engineer officers and engineer detachments were assigned to the sector commanders to supervise the construction workers and carry out demolition measures. Since only one construction engineer

battalion was available, General Reymann ordered two engineer battalions to be organized from Volkssturm troops trained for that purpose.

The construction manpower on hand consisted of some units of the Todt Organization and the Labor Service, the Volkssturm, and the civilian population. The total number of persons working on the positions amounted at the most to 70,000 on any one day. While that number seems small considering that Berlin contained over three million inhabitants, it must be remembered that until the very last the countless factories and workshops in and around the city were still working day and night. Moreover, the workers had to be transported to and from the construction areas every day. The city and suburban rail transit systems were already overtaxed and were often disrupted by the constant bombing raids. Many distant construction areas could not even be reached by rail, and gasoline for busses and trucks was not available. Efforts were made to utilize personnel from enterprises located near the positions under construction.

Only the Todt Organization and Reich Labor Service were well equipped. Most of the construction workers had to furnish their own tools. Small quantities of entrenching equipment could be obtained from the Rehagen-Klausdorf Engineer Depot. At first a few trenches and antitank ditches were dug with power shovels, but their use soon had to be discontinued because of lack of fuel.

Owing to the pressure of time and the shortage of building equipment and materials, it was out of the question to construct bunkers of reinforced concrete. Only very small quantities of mines and barbed wire were on hand.

The construction plans which could actually be carried out were limited largely to the following:

Along both the outer and inner ring, trenches with machine gun emplacements and splinterproof shelters or adjoining underground rooms were dug. For the most part the positions

A Soviet infantryman peers cautiously down a Berlin street.

had no depth. Streets in all sectors of the city were blocked by antitank obstacles. Antitank ditches were dug at a few important points along the outer ring. At main roads which might be used for incursions into the city a few mines were laid and barbed wire entanglements strung. Otherwise these were completely lacking. Rear and shift positions were built in many places between the city perimeter and the inner defense ring. Most of these detached positions resulted from the personal initiative of local Party leaders and showed a lack of co-ordinated planning and competent execution.

II. THE INDIVIDUAL POSITIONS

1. Outpost Area and Forward Defense Position.

Building the obstacle ring consisted merely in erecting road blocks at suitable points, mostly in inhabited localities. In conjunction with these, foxholes were dug as protection against tanks. Each road block was guarded by a security detachment of from thirty to forty Volkssturm men armed with infantry and antitank weapons.

All larger localities behind this obstacle ring were designated

The scene of destruction around the Brandenberg gate shortly after the official surrender.

as tactical strong points, which were to be defended to the last man. Since this measure could have had no tactical value, General Reymann by repeated protests to Hitler succeeded in having the plan abandoned.

Antitank obstacles were set up in every conceivable (and even inconceivable) place. Many of these hindered German troop movements and often had to be removed.

Few of the outpost area installations had any practical value. From the beginning the weak Volkssturm units were without heavy weapons, means of reconnaissance, and common leadership. They even lacked contact with one another. Only in exceptional instances did they delay the approach of the Russians for even a few hours. In most cases there was probably no defensive action at all, especially since the obstacles could usually be by-passed.

The forward defense position was inherently strong, since it took advantage of a favorable sector of terrain. The constructed defenses, however, were only those found in an ordinary field position. Luftwaffe personnel who had been made available in large numbers by Goering at the beginning of April, but who were unarmed and untrained in ground warfare, were assigned to hold this position, supplemented by Volkssturm troops.

This force apparently disintegrated at the approach of the Russians; there is no mention in any report of serious fighting for the forward defense position. Evidently the thirty battalions dispatched from Berlin on 21 April in the direction of this position were unable to reach it before the Russians, since on 22 April columns of Red troops were found west of this line, advancing along a broad front.

The forward defense position should have delayed the attacker for some time. This was not the case largely because of confusion in the chain of command. At the very moment that the advancing enemy reached this position, Hitler ordered the LVI Panzer Corps to take the offensive. All of its forces were massed for attack on both sides of the Berlin-Kuestrin railroad line, while to the north the Russians had a free hand. If the Ninth Army had been free to make its own decision, the LVI Panzer Corps would probably have been used to defend the forward defense position along a broad front. At the same time the right half of the Ninth Army, which had not been attacked, would have withdrawn from the Oder, sending as many of its elements as possible into the defense position to reinforce the hard-fighting left wing.

The Commander of the Defense Area, for his part, was unable to hold the forward defense position with the weak forces at his disposal. Its quick collapse resulted largely from the lack of a realistic and uniform command system.

2. Position Along the City Perimeter.
This position constituted the main line of resistance of the Berlin stronghold. It consisted largely of a continuous trench, with elaborations on the eastern and western flanks, where in both cases a second position was built behind the first.

The layout of the position was as follows: In the south, it ran first along the north bank of the Teltow Canal, then south of the canal from Lichterfelde to Johannistal. In the east the first position extended on either side of the Mueggelsee and then circled around Mahlsdorf; the second position followed the Gruenau - Herzberg railroad line. In the north, the line of defenses ran below the irrigated fields along the northern perimeter of the city past Weissensee and Niederschoenau, then parallel to the North Moat (a very minor obstacle) to the Tegeler See. In the west, it extended along the east bank of the Tegeler See and the Havel; the first position then continued along the western perimeter of the city past Spandau, Seeburg, Gross-Glienicke, and Sakrow (for the protection of the Gatow Airfield), and the second position along the east bank of the Havel lakes.

Behind this line lay the gun emplacements of the twenty permanent local batteries and the antiaircraft artillery that was not permanently emplaced.

The following excerpts from reports by men who took part in the fighting illustrate the condition of Berlin's defenses at the time contact was first made with the advancing enemy. Each report describes a company or battalion sector in one of the city's four quarters.

a. Teltow Canal near Klein-Machnow;
report of 1st Lieutenant von Reuss, commander of a
Volkssturm platoon:

Preparations for defense of the Teltow Canal included the construction of works along the northern bank and the organization of a bridge demolition team. A fire trench was laid out at a varying distance from the canal and machine gun emplacements were established 500-600 meters apart. Each emplacement was connected with a protected shelter by means of a communications trench.

The trenches led partly through marshy terrain and interfered greatly with troop movements. A machine gun emplacement, protected with cement slabs, was constructed on the grounds of an asbestos factory. There were no artillery emplacements to the rear, although two antiaircraft guns had been brought into position. A rocket projector had also been set up.

The only complete unit which figured in this sector was the Klein-Machnow Volkssturm Company, which was joined by a few stragglers from the Wehrmacht.

The platoon was armed with only one machine gun, of Czech manufacture, which went out of action after being fired only once. In addition, there were rifles of various foreign makes, including even some Italian Balilla rifles.

Of further interest is the fact, mentioned later in the report, that on the evening after the first encounter with the enemy the platoon adjacent to that of the writer went back to its quarters for the night and reappeared the next morning. Since the Russians attacked weakly here, the Volkssturm troops were able to hold this sector for two days.

**b. Sector east of Friedrichshagen (Mueggelsee);
report of Master Sergeant Guempe1, fortifications
construction superintendent:**

Sergeant Guempel and ten men from the cadre of the replacement battalion of the Gruenheide administrative unit were responsible after the middle of February for directing the construction of fortifications east of Friedrichshagen and to the north of the Mueggelsee, a sector about three kilometers in width. Manpower was recruited from the Friedrichshagen population and from workers in the local factories. As many as five hundred workers a day were provided. A continuous trench was dug and permanent emplacements were prepared. The construction of shelters was begun under supervision of a building expert from Friedrichshagen, although none were completed before the start of the fighting.

It had been planned to occupy the position with a force of 250 men, comprising elements of the replacement battalion and Volkssturm troops. With the approach of the Russians, the force holding the position disintegrated and the position was left virtually unmanned. Only the battalion commander and about twenty-five men offered resistance. The defenders were overcome, after which Sergeant Guempel and his group tried to collect stragglers.

c. Sector east of the Tegeler See; report of Major Schwark, commander of a plant protection battalion:

The position sector was bounded on the left by the northern tip of the Tegeler See, from where it extended to the right along the Tegeler Run, also called the North Moat. This moat held little water and was more a line along which to build fortifications than an actual obstacle itself. The position consisted of a shallow fire trench, without barbed wire or mines.

The battalion commander had been familiarized with the terrain and had participated in two map exercises. The position was occupied by the plant protection battalion, which comprised four understrength companies armed with rifles, hand grenades, and a few Panzerfaeuste. Most of the men were veterans of World War I and, because of their service with plant protection units, were accustomed to order and discipline. The Russians avoided a frontal attack, using infiltration instead, especially at night; such tactics were aided by the poor visibility afforded by the terrain. Particular trouble was caused by roof-top snipers in front of and behind the German lines. Nevertheless, it was still possible to keep the men together. When the battalion was almost surrounded after three days of fighting, it withdrew and occupied a new position in the Wittler bakery plant, where the writer was seriously wounded.

d. Gatow sector; report of Major Komorowski, commander of a composite battalion:

The battalion, as part of a regiment, defended a section of the first position, located along the western perimeter of the Gatow Airfield, which was to be protected against attack from the west.

Captured German soldiers stream through the streets of Berlin. Note the extreme youth of the foreground figures.

If the first position were lost, the troops were to cross the Wannsee in boats lying in readiness in order to occupy the second position along the east bank of the lake.

The position consisted of a well-built, continuous trench. The battalion was composed of construction and Volkssturm troops, none of whom had had combat experience. They were armed with captured rifles and a few machine guns, and had only a limited supply of ammunition. The infantry was supported by an 88-mm antiaircraft gun battery and a heavy infantry gun platoon, although the latter unit had never fired its weapons. Support was also received from the garrison of the Zoo Flak Tower. On the evening of the first day of battle all the Volkssturm troops deserted, and the gap was filled only by recruiting stragglers. In two days of fighting all the defenders were either killed or captured.

The position along the city perimeter, which formed the main line of resistance of the Berlin stronghold, had little over-all value. For long stretches it consisted only of a fire trench, without support in front or behind. Nowhere was the position manned by well co-ordinated, battle-tried troops. The loosely organized, makeshift units were inadequately armed and varied greatly in their will to fight. It is astounding that in many places the Russians allowed themselves to be held back for several days by the resistance of a few valiant men. Wherever the enemy made a serious effort to push forward, the position fell with the first onslaught. The enemy did not take full advantage of such successes, however, but changed over to a hesitant and methodical attack procedure. As a result, the various intermediate and switch positions halted their advance time and again. Once past the outer defenses, the enemy encountered the experienced and well-armed troops of the LVI Panzer Corps, who made full use of the prepared positions and the terrain in between to offer strong resistance.

3. Position Along the Town Circuit Railroad and the Innermost Defenses.

The value of the town circuit railroad lay in its offering the defenders a clear line of defense. The fortifications constructed here were similar to those along the perimeter of the city, although because of the hard soil continuous trenches generally had not been dug. The position consisted primarily of permanent individual emplacements for three or four men. Plans had also been made to fortify the streets behind the position; this was done according to available means and individual initiative. These preparations are described in a report by a former Volkssturm battalion commander, Heinrich Bath:

The Volkssturm battalion, organized in Charlottenburg West, was to serve as a reserve for another Volkssturm battalion, which was drawn up along the city circuit railroad. Defense fortifications were to be built along the street behind the forward battalion. The reserve battalion had a strength of eight hundred men. Weapons and tools, especially entrenching tools, were lacking. Many of the men had no proper work clothes. The battalion was under the orders of Party District Headquarters I on Wittenbergplatz. At the same time, the battalion was also subordinate to a military sector headquarters. This situation often caused confusion in command.

First of all, fixed and movable tank obstacles were constructed. The three main thoroughfares in the battalion sector were provided with stationary concrete obstacles with movable middle sections to allow the passage of streetcars and other vehicles. The openings were closed after dark and were always strongly guarded. At night all traffic was suspended. Side streets were provided with stationary obstacles which completely blocked vehicle traffic and left only a narrow opening on one side for pedestrians. These obstacles - some twelve barricades, each three meters high - consisted of beams and steel girders rammed into the street bed and covered with heaps of rubble.

To cover the streets, machine-gun emplacements were set up on upper stories. Passageways were constructed from the cellars into the street as posts from which to attack tanks with Panzerfaeuste. Cellars were converted into shelters and connected with one another so that troop movements could be carried out under cover. The roofs were also prepared for battle; sniper posts were set up and passages for access were devised.

As a result of the extensive construction work training was largely neglected, although lectures were given to bolster morale.

Shortly before the battle the battalion received about a hundred rifles. During the fighting only about sixty men remained at their posts, the greater number having returned to their homes.

Many sections of the position along the city circuit railroad, the inner defense, and the numerous switch positions, were made ready in the manner described above. The extent of the work accomplished depended entirely on the competence and initiative of those directing the construction. Works of this kind in a large city make possible very strong resistance, provided they are occupied by troops determined to fight. In Berlin some positions were stoutly defended, while others fell into Russian hands almost without a struggle.

4. The Flak Towers.

The Zoo, Humboldthain, and Friedrichshain flak towers, as well as the flak control tower (without guns) had been built during the period of the air attacks. They served as antiaircraft gun emplacements and air defense command posts and at the same time as giant air raid shelters for protection of the population. With their own light and water installations and large supplies of ammunition and food, these structures were capable of sheltering fifteen thousand persons in addition to the military garrison. During the fighting they were filled with wounded, deserters, and civilians, so that their normal capacity was probably far exceeded.

Because of their location and construction, no thought had been given to utilizing the flak towers in the ground fighting. No embrasures existed and no entrance defenses had been constructed. The surrounding area fell within the blind angle of the guns emplaced on the platforms and terraces of the towers. Nevertheless, the towers held out very well in the ensuing battle. The antiaircraft artillery played a successful part in the ground fighting, even in the suburbs of the city. None of the towers was pierced by bombs or direct hits by heavy artillery. In attacking the Zoo flak tower, Russian tanks attempted to fire into the windows, which were protected only by sheets of armored plate. Only a few lower-story windows were hit; the enemy guns could not be elevated to reach the upper stories. In the rooms where shells exploded, heavy casualties were caused by flying fragments of concrete, since the walls had not been faced.

The close defense of the towers was conducted from field positions set up around them. The Humboldthain and Friedrichshain flak towers held out for days after being completely surrounded. The Zoo flak and flak control towers also did not surrender until after the general capitulation. At that time the antiaircraft artillery of the Zoo tower was still intact, whereas that of the Friedrichshain tower had been put out of action by bomb hits. The Friedrichshain tower surrendered as early as 30 April, partly because in that sector the Russians drove the German population before them as they attacked.

III. PLANS FOR DEMOLITION

l. Bridges.

Preparations had been made to blow up all bridges and numerous overpasses in Berlin. Bitter quarrels subsequently arose between those who, like the Commander of the Defense Area, advocated military necessity, and those who wished to prevent the demolitions in the interest of the population. Reich Minister Speer, especially, did his utmost to moderate the extent of the destruction. The question was vitally significant not only because of the need for traffic routes, but above all because the water and sewerage mains lay under the bridges. Speer succeeded in obtaining from Hitler an order whereby a number of particularly important bridges were to be saved.

The degree to which the demolitions were carried out during the battle varied. Some of the bridges were only damaged, so that they could still be crossed by infantry and, after repairs, by tanks and other vehicles.

According to an investigation made by Colonel Roos, of the 248 bridges in Berlin 120 were destroyed and 9 damaged. (See Sketch 4 overleaf)

Only a few of the overpasses were blown up, apparently for lack of explosives.

2. Subway and City Transit Line Tunnels.

The network of subway and city transit line tunnels could be used for covered movements by both friendly and enemy troops. In case of necessity they could be blocked at various points by

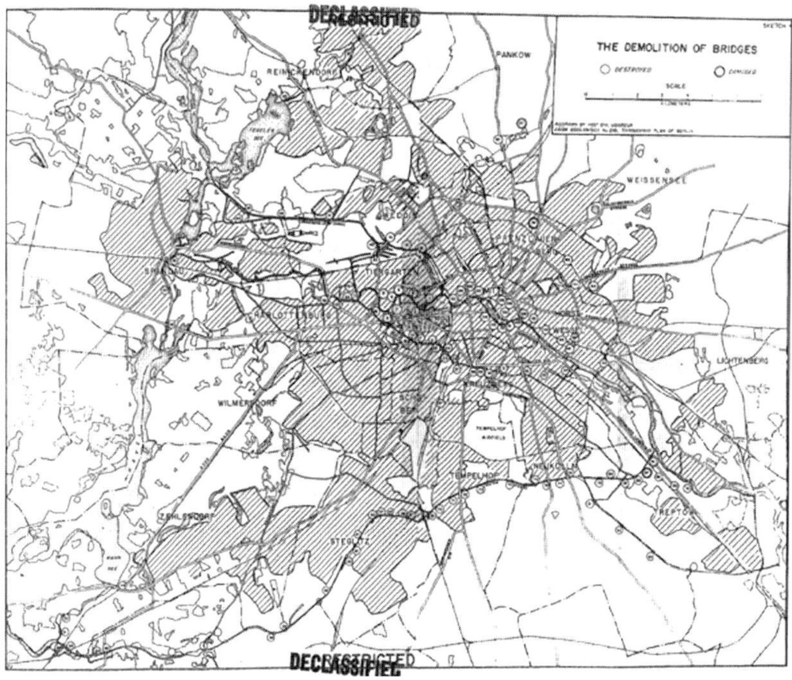

Sketch 4 - The demolition of bridges

setting off explosive charges that had already been planted.

In the course of the battle the city transit line tunnel under the Landwehr Canal was blown up, after which it filled with water. It could not be determined at whose orders this measure was carried out. With the blowing up of the Ebert Bridge (east of the Weidendamm Bridge) the city transit line tunnel there was also destroyed, although this was apparently unintentional. Because of these and other explosions, water flowed into large parts of the subway and city transit line tunnels in the heart of the city. (See Sketch 5 opposite)

It could not be proven that any appreciable loss of life resulted from the flooding of these tunnels, but it can be seriously doubted that it was justified by military necessity. *[It was common talk among the Allied occupation forces that hundreds of bodies were later recovered from these tunnels.]*

The tunnel leading from the Zoo railroad station (Bahnhof

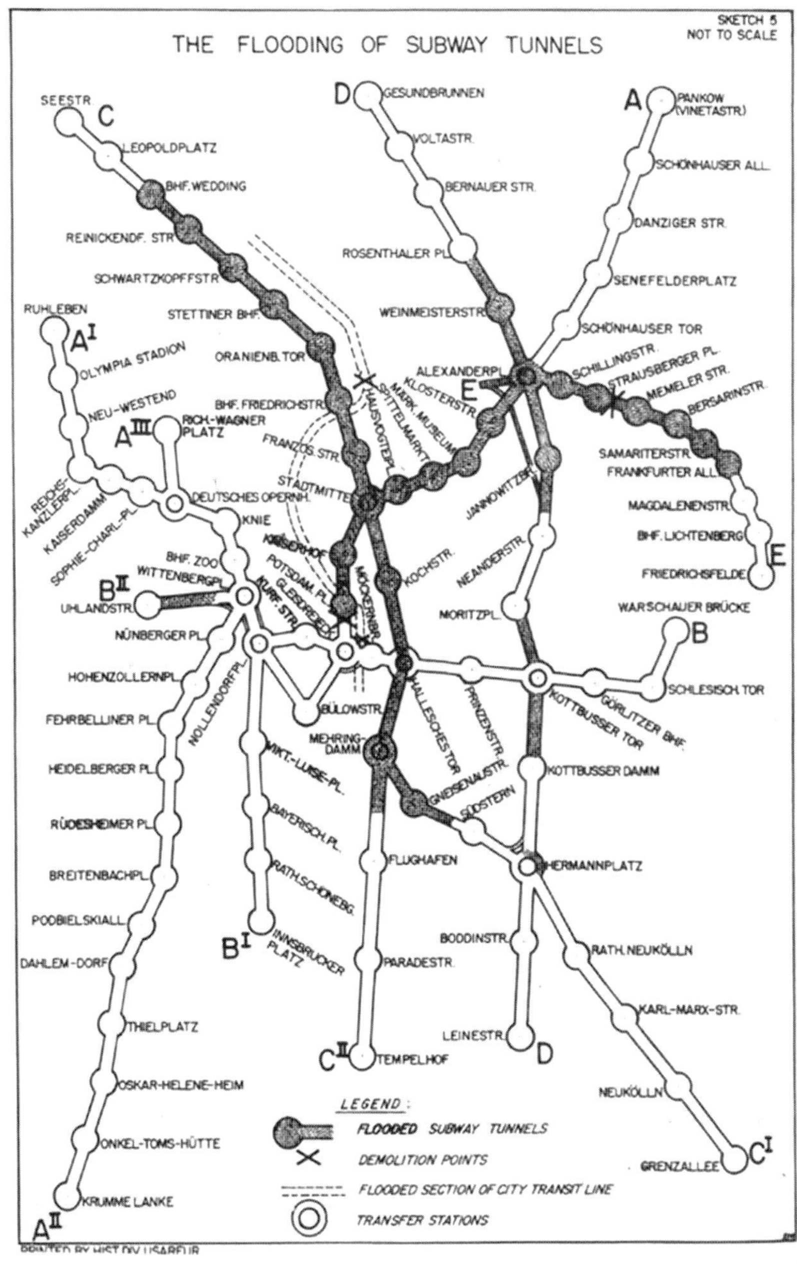

Sketch 5 - the flooding of subway tunnels

Zoo) to Ruhleben was heavily used by troops and civilians trying to break out toward the west.

3. Destruction of Business and Industrial Installations.

On 19 March Hitler had issued instructions for demolitions which came to be known as the "scorched earth" order:

1. All military, transportation, communications, industrial, and supply installations and all real property within the territory of the Reich which the enemy can make use of in any way either now or in the foreseeable future for the pursuance of his war effort are to be destroyed.

2. The following authorities are responsible for carrying out these demolitions:

    a. The military command agencies for all military objectives including transportation, and communications installations.

    b. The Gauleiters and Reich Defense Commissioners for all industrial and supply facilities and other real property. Military agencies will furnish all necessary assistance.

Since these measures would have deprived the population of the means of survival, the demolition plan that had been worked out for Berlin was submitted by the Army High Command (Inspectorate of Fortresses) to Reich Minister Speer with the request that he persuade Hitler to change the order. The supply installations of Berlin were subsequently excluded from the demolition plan. The engineer commander of the Defense Area was instructed to discuss the plan with the appropriate Berlin official, Assistant Mayor Hettasch.

IV. BUILD-UP OF SIGNAL COMMUNICATIONS

Provision could not be made for a military telephone network for the agencies conducting the defense, since no materials or signal units were available. Only a few signal personnel were attached to the military offices. Thus the Defense Area was forced to fall back on the civilian telephone network. In addition, the antiaircraft units had their own communications network.

While the postal system functioned remarkably well in view

A Soviet tank crew observe their handiwork; Berlin 1945.

of the constant bombing, there was no possibility of directing the subordinate troops efficiently through postal channels, since they provided no rapid means of transmitting messages. The Defense Area had no radio equipment. Battle reports of the permanent local units expressly indicate that contacts with one another and with superior agencies depended on the use of messengers. It sometimes took hours to deliver a message a few hundred meters through the rubble-littered streets under enemy fire.

The lack of means of communication undoubtedly contributed to the chaos in the issuance of orders for the conduct of the battle and the distribution of supplies. The LVI Panzer Corps, to the extent that its units still possessed their own signal equipment, was less handicapped in this respect.

V. SUMMARY

The entire build-up of defenses in Berlin was characterized by lack of specialized personnel and facilities of all kinds. Despite all efforts by the city's skilled commander, General Reymann, Berlin could only be provided with a number of field positions of moderate strength. These acquired real combat value only in the heart of the city, where more favorable conditions were offered by the blocks of rubble and devastated buildings.

The city's designation as a "fortified place" was pure fiction. The build-up of the defenses could not be adapted to a fighting force capable of effective defense, since no such force was available. Instead, preparations were carried out only with regard to the terrain features; no one asked whether the necessary defenders would be available at the critical moment. In many places the weak security troops of the Volkssturm put up no resistance at all. Even if they had shown the greatest courage, however, they would never have succeeded in their mission. On the whole, the positions had only a delaying effect, largely because their very existence caused the Russians to proceed slowly and cautiously.

The resistance encountered by the Russians in Berlin from 23 April to 1 May was not based wholly on the prepared positions. To a large extent, the defenders, especially the LVI Panzer Corps, clung tenaciously to the numerous possibilities for defense offered by the rubble and ruins of the great city.

5. PLANNING FOR THE DEFENSE FORCES

1. GENERAL.

It has been pointed out that the defense forces originally planned for were wholly inadequate and that it was necessary to bring in frontline troops to defend the sprawling city. Planned operations went hand in hand with improvisation. The organizational difficulties which resulted can be seen from a study of the chain of command.

In this chapter an attempt will be made to indicate what forces were actually at hand. While complete data is lacking, probably not a single post included any units at full strength.

In addition to permanent local troops and the LVI Panzer Corps, a number of improvised forces and alert units were organized in Berlin proper. Units were also poured into Berlin at the last minute by the Army, Luttwaffe, Navy, Party, SS, Police, and Labor Service. These troops were carried in by train, motor vehicle, transport plane, or moved in on foot. Some forces either did not reach Berlin, or else arrived only in small numbers. Others passed through the city on their way to the forward defense position, while still others remained outside the city and were later forced to withdraw. Many groups moved quietly out of Berlin to the west. In addition to the divisions of the LVI Panzer Corps, remnants of other front-line units were swept into Berlin.

The troops listed here do not constitute forces of any considerable size, but do represent a large number of different unit designations. If it were possible to draw up a complete list of all units involved, a false picture of the situation would result

On the outskirts of Berlin the Volkssturm dig in and prepare to face the Soviet onslaught.

from the discrepancy between actual and authorized strength. Consideration must also be given to actual combat value. Nevertheless, it is hoped that the following survey of units making up the defense forces provides a useful over-all estimate.

II. PERMANENT LOCAL FORCES

1. Staff of the Commander of the Berlin Defense Area.

This staff was set up at the beginning of February 1945 by Deputy Headquarters, III Corps, in the III Wehrkreis Building on Hohenzollerndamm. Mention has already been made of the successive occupants of the post of commander.

The staff was constituted as follows:

- Chief of Staff : Colonel (GSC)
- Senior Chief of Operations: Major (GSC) Sprotte
- Chief Supply Officer: Major Weiss
- Artillery Commander: Lt. Colonel Platho
- Signal Commander: Lt. Colonel Fricke
- Engineer Commander: Colonel (GSC) Lobeck

On 25 April, as the Russians were approaching the

Hohenzollerndamm, the staff moved to the bunker on Bendlerstrasse. The Artillery Commander had established his command post in the flak control tower near the Zoo.

2. The Volkssturm.

Numerically, the Volkssturm was by far the strongest component of the defense forces. Generalleutnant Reymann listed its strength at 92 battalions (60,000 men), of which about 30 battalions, according to his report, were moved into the forward defense position. Remnants of these forces may have been swept back into Berlin.

a. Formation and Organization. The Volkssturm was set up in the fall of 1944 under Party auspices by the Reich Defense Commissioner, and was not a component part of the Army. Its mission was to protect rear areas against minor enemy infiltrations or break-throughs and against parachute troops, to serve as security forces for the manning of rear positions, and to engage in the building of fortifications. Originally Volkssturm troops were not to be committed at the front within the framework of the Army. Their mission could be compared to that of the British Home Guards.

Once the enemy had set foot on Reich territory, the emergency situation at the front made it necessary to utilize the Volkssturm in the front lines in ever increasing numbers, though it was by no means fit for such service. With front-line commitment, difficulties resulting from divided authority immediately arose. Undoubtedly the Volkssturm should have been organized as a component part of the Army, a plan for which Generaloberst Guderian had tried vainly to secure approval.

In Berlin the Volkssturm was divided into two categories, designated Volkssturm I and Volkssturm II; Volkssturm I had only a few weapons while Volkssturm II had none at all. Volkssturm II was intended as a manpower reserve for Volkssturm 1. The use of these forces in Berlin was planned so that Volkssturm I would occupy a forward position - for instance, along the city perimeter - while Volkssturm II would be close behind along a second position to serve as a security force and as a reserve for replacing casualties. This plan was actually followed in some sectors.

The Volkssturm was composed of men who could bear arms in emergency, but who were not physically fit for active duty. They ranged in age to sixty years and over, the majority being in upper age brackets. Among members of the Volkssturm were men who had had no service and veterans of World War I. These latter often distinguished themselves by their sense of duty. The Volkssturm was broken down into companies and battalions. Unit commanders were appointed by the Party; hence they were partly Party functionaries and partly reserve officers. In one instance a staff officer who had been dismissed by Hitler found himself a private under a commander who had never before held a military rank.

The Volkssturm was organized on a local basis; all the male inhabitants of a locality or section of a city were grouped in one battalion. When not actually fighting, the men pursued their normal occupation during the day, lived with their families, and took their meals at home.

The strength of the companies and battalions depended on the number of eligible inhabitants in each locality; in Berlin each battalion comprised between 600 and 1,500 men.

b. Training. Before being assigned to duty Volkssturm members received training on week-ends or in the evenings from about 1700 to 1900 hours unless they were employed in building fortifications. Training was given in the use of rifles and machine guns, wherever such weapons were available. Only in a few isolated instances did any practice firing take place. The commanders received instruction and were familiarized with their local combat duties. Three-day courses in SA training camps were also offered. The degree or training varied greatly

Soviet dive bombers range at will over the suburbs of Berlin.

but was generally insufficient.

c. Equipment and Weapons. Members of the Volkssturm wore civilian clothes with arm bands. Their weapons were as varied as they were inadequate. Troops of Volkssturm I were issued rifles, and to some extent also machine guns. These included many European models, among them Czech, Belgian, and Italian. A very few battalions were equipped with German rifles. The supply of ammunition amounted in many cases to five rounds per rifle; in some cases, however, the ammunition on hand did not fit any rifle. No heavy weapons and only a small number of Panzerfaeuste were available. Apart from the aforementioned thirty battalions, which were relatively well armed, the bulk of the Volkssturm was practically defenseless. None or the Volkssturm units were issued signal equipment.

Rations for the Volkssturm were provided by the population even during the fighting, but these were usually inadequate. The Volkssturm troops had no field kitchens or ration supply vehicles of their own, so that outside of their own home area they found themselves without rations.

d. Combat value. Against the well equipped and battle-tried troops of the Red Army, the combat value of the battalions remaining in Berlin was almost nil, in spite of the will that was frequently present. This does not mean that detachments of Volkssturm men did not in many instances put up a gallant fight. When it came time for serious fighting, however, the bulk of the Volkssturm simply stayed at home. In some cases entire unarmed battalions were dismissed by clear-sighted military commanders. However, in places where the Russians attacked either feebly or not at all Volkssturm unites were able to occupy a sector or delay the enemy advance for some days.

3. Local Defense Forces, Schools, Replacement Units, and Plant Protection Troops.

a. Local Defense Forces. At the beginning of January Berlin organized a number of local defense battalions, composed of men subject to military service who were not fit for front-line duty. They were armed with rifles and a few machine guns, mostly captured weapons, and were issued a small amount of ammunition. Their mission was to guard bridges, railroad stations, military camps, and war prisoners.

Some of these battalions were shifted at the beginning of February to the Oder front, while others moved the prisoners of war who had been put to work in and around Berlin toward the west. Only a small number of companies and battalions fought in Berlin. Their combat value was very slight.

b. Schools. An ordnance technician school and an ordnance officer candidate school were located in Berlin. Courses had been discontinued and the permanent staffs assigned to the southern perimeter of the city. The permanent staffs of the schools in the surrounding area - at Zossen, Wuensdorf, Doeberitz, Gatow, and other districts - were for the most part assigned to combat duty outside Berlin.

c. Replacement Troops. The replacement troops of the Army had all been used in February to build up the fresh contingents which were thrown into the Oder line. At the beginning of April,

Wermacht-Heer prisoners being marched off to face an uncertain future in captivity. Many would not return, others were held as forced labourers for 10 years or more.

however, a fairly large number of replacement troops from the Luftwaffe were placed at the disposal of Army Group Vistula. Because they lacked training in ground fighting and were inadequately armed, the latter assigned them to rear positions and to the forward defense position. Their combat value was negligible.

d. Plant Protection Troops. The large industrial firms and the postal and railway systems each had at their disposal a few companies of plant protection troops, armed with rifles. They were consolidated into battalions and assigned to the battle lines, where they had little combat value.

4. Alert Units.

Personnel of the military agencies and staffs were organized into "alert companies." This designation was also given to units composed of convalescents and numerous stragglers, which were set up by the military police and the straggler interception patrols. These soldiers were poorly armed, and their fighting spirit was low. The stragglers, especially, could only be held together by the application of rigorous punitive measures. Toward the end of the battle thousands of soldiers unwilling to fight were found in cellars and bunkers. Again it was shown that it is not the anonymous soldier who fights battles, but the soldier who preserves his identity through close association with his comrades and superiors.

Waffen-SS. The SS units thrown into Berlin were organized under SS Brigadefuehrer Mohnke into a well-armed force of high combat value and good morale. The brigade, comprising several thousand men, was assigned to the government sector.

6. Permanent Local Artillery Forces.

When Lt. Colonel Platho assumed his duties as Artillery Commander of the Defense Area on 19 March 1945, he found seven light batteries and seven heavy batteries of artillery on hand. All the guns were of foreign manufacture. Between 100 and 120 rounds of ammunition per battery were available. At first there were no prime movers or vehicles, but later two prime movers were located.

Among the battery commanders there were three paymaster

officials, who were not even from the artillery, but had merely completed a short artillery course in which each had fired a gun once. The gun crews were made up of soldiers from all branches of the service, few of whom were artillerymen, and of members of the Volkssturm. There was no battalion or regimental staff.

A telephone line between the observation point and the batteries was operated by antiaircraft artillery women auxiliaries. Orders were transmitted by telephone through the use of the communications facilities of the nearby flak positions. There was no other telephone equipment and not a single radio set.

The first firing of live ammunition ordered by Lt. Colonel Platho was discontinued because it endangered the observation post.

In the short time available the artillery commander increased the number of batteries to twenty by making use of the dismantled training guns found in the Ordnance Technician and Ordnance Officer Candidate Schools. A few artillery officers were made available, and were assigned either to the batteries or as liaison officers to the sector command headquarters, in place of the missing battalion staffs. Crews of the German-made guns consisted of former search-light operators who had never fired artillery. Ammunition for the German guns was no more plentiful than for those of foreign manufacture.

In addition to the artillery, a few rocket projectors were set up along the most important avenues of approach. While they were fired with good psychological effect, each projector had only enough ammunition for one salvo.

7. Antitank Defenses.

One relatively battle-worthy unit was a tank demolition battalion composed of three companies and equipped with Volkswagens, each of which was fitted with a rack for six antitank rockets. It could not be determined whether this battalion was employed in Berlin or whether it was moved out to the forward defense position.

The other antitank defenses consisted of the antiaircraft installations that were committed to ground action and the various means of close-range anti tank combat.

8. Antiaircraft Artillery.

The 1st Flak Division, under Generalmajor Sydow, was stationed in Berlin. Combat headquarters were located at the antiaircraft control post near the Zoo.

There were four antiaircraft artillery regiments with four or five battalions (20-mm and 128-mm guns). A few batteries with older guns of German and foreign make were used as barrage batteries. Before the start of the fighting a searchlight regiment was dispersed throughout the city.

The air defenses centered around the three flak towers, located near the Zoo, in Friedrichshain, and in Humboldthain respectively. The batteries in the towers consisted of six 128-mm guns each. On the terrace of each tower were placed twelve 20-mm guns. Ammunition was adequate.

During the fighting the flak towers formed vital centers for the artillery defenses. The towers were connected by underground telephone cables.

The other antiaircraft batteries were to be deployed along the city perimeter position. This plan failed in many instances because the guns were mounted fast in concrete. Furthermore, the Berlin antiaircraft units were not trained for ground action. In one instance, witnessed by General Reymann, practice fire aimed at targets on the Mueggelsee did not even hit the lake.

Accordingly, the combat value of the antiaircraft units distributed along the city perimeter was slight. In many instances they were quickly overcome by the Russian tanks and artillery. One antiaircraft group, consisting of two battalions deployed around Tempelhof Airfield and to the south of it kept the enemy engaged for two days. When the Russians broke through on either side, the guns that were still serviceable were blown up and the remnants of the gun crews were thrown into action as infantry.

Keitel (centre) signs the official surrender of Berlin. With the Nazi-Soviet pact to dismember Poland conveniently overlooked, he was later to hang at Nuremberg for his part in bringing about World War II.

9. The Hitler Youth.

Besides participating in the fighting as flak auxiliaries and in small groups attached to the regular troops and the Volkssturm, the Hitler Youth were organized into their own battalions. Some battalions were combined to form the Axmann Brigade and were engaged in antitank operations east of the forward defense position. They were armed with rifles and Panzerfaeuste.

The total strength of the Hitler Youth in Berlin is not known. In the western part of the city some battalions were fighting under the Reich Youth Leader in the radio tower sector and near Pichelsdorf, where they held a bridgehead. Enthusiastic fighting spirit only partly made up for lack of weapons and training.

III. THE LVI PANZER CORPS

The LVI Panzer Corps, commanded by General der Artillerie Weidling, was moved to Berlin on 24 April 1945. The corps chief of staff was Colonel (GSC) von Duffing. Other staff officers included Major (GSC) Knabe, Chief of Operations; Major (GSC) Wagner, Chief Supply Officer; and Colonel

Woehlermann, commander of the corps artillery.

The following troop units were brought into Berlin under the corps' command:

1. The 20th Panzer Grenadier Division. This division had suffered heavy casualties in the battle on the Oder. Its strength and combat value were very low.

2. Panzer Division "Muencheberg" (Commander: Generalmajor Mummert). Reorganized in Doeberitz in spring under the designation Panzer Division "Doeberitz," this division was later renamed because of confusion with Infantry Division "Doeberitz." Following severe fighting west of the Oder, the division arrived in Berlin with only about half its authorized strength and not more than twenty tanks. It was battle-weary but still fit for action.

3. The 18th Panzer Grenadier Division (Commander: Generalmajor Rauch). Rehabilitated in spring of 1945, this division was about equal to Panzer Division "Muencheberg" in strength and combat value.

4. SS Panzer Grenadier Division "Nordland" (Commander: SS Gruppenfuehrer Ziegler). Complemented with volunteers from Scandinavia, it was inferior in strength and combat value to Panzer Division "Muencheberg."

5. The 408th Volks Artillerie Corps. This unit was composed of four light artillery battalions, two heavy artillery battalions with Russian 152-mm guns, and one howitzer battalion with four howitzers. About 60 percent of the artillery pieces were brought to Berlin with almost no ammunition.

6. Remnants of other combat units, including the 9th Parachute Division and SS Panzer Grenadier Division "Nederland." These units were all low in fighting strength and combat value.

IV. FLYING UNITS

During the first days of the fighting in and around Berlin, units of the German Luftwaffe went into action a number of times in formations of from forty to sixty planes. They took part in the operations in accordance with direct instructions from the Chief of the Luftwaffe General Staff.

V. SUMMARY

1. Fighting Power.

Numerically, a rough survey of all troops available after the encirclement of the city gives the following picture: The LVI Panzer Corps was equal to about two divisions, the Waffen SS forces to about half a division, and all other forces in the city to from two to three divisions, a total of about four to five divisions.

The city contained an estimated 60,000 soldiers and from fifty to sixty tanks. *[The figures given by the Russians are highly exaggerated. General Bazarine, in the Revue de defense nationale, 1951, p.425, has estimated the strength of the German forces at 180,000 men. This figure may correspond to authorized strength, but not to actual strength in the field. The great number of prisoners captured after the surrender can be explained by the fact that a large number of soldiers did not take part in the fighting and that at first the Russians took prisoner everyone who was in uniform, including railway officials, city policemen, and members of the Labor Service.]*

There is no data from which to estimate the number of casualties sustained; they were high owing to the nature of street fighting.

The "other forces" estimated above as corresponding to between two and three divisions were largely splinter units of various types. Volkssturm companies, alert units, members of the Hitler Youth, parties of stragglers from the front, and SS units were to be found side by side and intermingled, without any over-all organization. A Latvian battalion in this category immediately went over to the enemy. The adjacent unit was often completely unknown and just as often unreliable. As a result the

This famous image taken shortly after the fighting had ended was staged twice for Soviet cameras.

Russians repeatedly reached positions to the rear of valiantly fighting units. There were no command communications channels. Messengers often took hours to proceed a few hundred meters through the rubble-strewn streets. There were no heavy weapons, and only here and there a single assault gun or antiaircraft installation. The procurement of ammunition and rations depended on chance and the ingenuity of the unit commander.

2. Fighting Spirit.

Fighting spirit was sustained by fear of the Russians and by the hope, cleverly nurtured by Goebbel's propaganda machine, for a shift in front by the Western Allies and for the launching of German relief attacks. On the other hand, the excessive hardships, the prolongation of the uninterrupted fighting, and the desperate over-all situation produced fatigue and lethargy among the troops. The nervous strain exceeded the limit of endurance.

Toward the end of the battle the man who still held a weapon in his hand did so either from a sense of duty or with the courage of despair. A great many examples of heroic resistance were shown by troops of all types - regular army, SS, Volkssturm, Hitler Youth, and others. The number of those who regarded surrender as treason and those who as fanatical Nazis actually continued fighting was by no means small. Thus it was that, when the capitulation was announced, parlementaires as well as Colonel Woehlermann and other officers were threatened with death.

The conduct of the civilian population on the whole was exemplary. However, a few veterans of the battle reported that in the eastern sector of the city, where there have always been a large number of Communists, some elements of the population fraternized with the Russians and even took up arms to fight on the Russian side.

6. SUPPLY

I. AMMUNITION

According to a report by Chief Ordnance Technician Schmidt, there existed in Berlin at the beginning of the fighting three large ammunition depots: Depot Martha in the Hasenheide People's Park (southern sector of Berlin), Depot Mars in the Grunewald Park on the Teufelssee (western sector), and Depot Monika in the Jungfernheide People's Park (northwest sector). Before the fighting these depots were eighty per cent full. Smaller quantities of ammunition were stored in the Tiergarten area.

With the threatened approach of the Russians from the north, two thirds of the ammunition in Depot Monika was transported by horse team to Depot Mars. Depots Mars and Martha fell into Russian hands on 25 April.

When questioned explicitly on the subject, the Artillery Commander of the Defense Area, Lt. Colonel Platho claimed that he had no knowledge of the existence of the above-mentioned depots. The reason for this could not be determined

Russian infantry supported by tanks battle their way through Berlin.

In the ruins of Berlin, a Russian tank man seeks targets for his heavy machine gun.

by the author. On the one hand, reports from all the combat elements indicate a chronic shortage of ammunition, which, in fact, was a characteristic feature of the battle for Berlin. On the other hand, there is no reason to doubt the very thorough and clear report of Chief Technician Schmidt, a member of the ammunition administration staff, especially since the existence of the depots is also mentioned in another report.

It is possible that in the depots there was no ammunition for the weapons of foreign make, which constituted the greater part of the armament of the Volkssturm and the permanent local artillery. There is also a possibility that these depots were closed off until the city was surrounded, in order to prevent the ammunition from being diverted to other fronts; and that shortly after the encirclement of the city and the entry of the LVI Panzer Corps (with German weapons), the depots were captured by the enemy. These attempted explanations must be supplemented by a reference to the command situation as described in Chapter 3.

The shortage of ammunition was a practical reality, despite the fact that well-stocked depots were initially available. This was another indication of the incomplete and unco-ordinated defense planning. Numerous small depots in the heart of the city would have served better than the three large ones in the outlying sectors.

II. GASOLINE

No figures could be obtained for the supply of gasoline on hand. It was so limited, however, that not only was it necessary to cease operation of the power shovels but impossible to provide motorized transportation for the movement of troops and construction workers. In certain instances tanks had to be dug into position for lack of fuel.

III. FOOD

In addition to the civilian food warehouses, there were also well-stocked Wehrmacht ration supply depots in Berlin. Plans for the systematic distribution of these supplies were disrupted by the rapid course of events.

One large Wehrmacht ration supply depot was located on the south bank of the Teltow Canal near Klein-Machnow, outside of the outer defense ring. No steps were taken to remove the supplies from this depot or to assure their quick distribution. On

A Panther V tank dug in on a Berlin street provided a strong-point during the street fighting. Judging from the large number of spent shell cases this survivor of the Panzerwaffe put up a very fierce resistance.

the contrary, even when the first Russian tank was only a few hundred meters away, the army official administering the depot refused to let rations be distributed to the Volkssturm troops on the north bank of the canal because a regulation issue certificate had not been filled out. At the last moment the supplies were set on fire, careful preparations for their destruction having been made well in advance.

In many places, therefore, the troops were short of rations, while in other instances they helped themselves from the depots located in their assigned areas.

IV. WATER

Because of the breakdown in the public water system, shortages of water occurred in many places during the fighting. It was possible, however, for the troops to supply their needs by drawing water from wells and from the watercourses in the heart of the city.

7. MEASURES ON BEHALF OF THE CIVILIAN POPULATION

The exact number of civilians in Berlin at the time of the city's encirclement is not known. The original population of 4.5 million had been reduced to about 2.5 million by the large-scale evacuation of women with children and old people, during the severe air raids of 1943. However, a great many of the evacuees who had been removed to areas east of the city returned to Berlin when the Russians invaded the territory of the Reich. Innumerable refugees fleeing from the eastern provinces were also stranded in the city.

An evacuation of the population in anticipation of the defense and possible encirclement of the city was never considered. People were encouraged to stay where they were, since it would have been impossible to assemble everybody in a safe place. On the other hand, those who wished to leave of their own accord were free to do so, provided they were not bound by duties in offices or factories or with the Volkssturm. Thus the number of inhabitants at the time of the encirclement of the city may have totaled between 3 and 3.5 million.

To assure food for the population well stocked warehouses were located throughout the city. Notwithstanding the deliberate destruction by Germans and damage caused by the fighting, there must have been a large food supply on hand at the time of the capitulation. Despite wide-spread plundering by Russian troops and liberated foreign workers, it was possible for important components of the Russian Army, as well as the civilian population, to live for months on this reserve, although admittedly the population received only the barest essentials.

The reports disagree over whether or not advance rations for

German prisoners are marched past a heavy ISU 152mm Soviet assault gun.

several weeks were distributed to the population. Apparently this practical measure was carried out in some parts of the city and not in others. Even during the fighting long lines of people stood in front of food stores waiting to buy rations.

A particular problem was the feeding of the approximately 120,000 infants in Berlin. When questioned by General Reymann about this matter, Hitler denied that there were such children in the city. This answer is an indication of Hitler's ignorance of conditions in his own capital, which he saw only as it looked from the Fuehrer Bunker. Dr. Goebbels told General Reymann that there was sufficient canned milk on hand and that, in case of encirclement, the milk cows in the surrounding areas would be brought into Berlin. He could give no answer, however, to the question of providing feed for the cows.

The plan for feeding the population was quickly rendered ineffectual by the fact that most of the food supply depots were located in outlying districts, which were occupied by the Russians early in the fighting.

Some provision was made for assuring a supply of water, even after the disruption of the water mains, by the construction of wells and fire fighting reservoirs.

8. CONCLUDING OBSERVATIONS

Running like a continuous thread through the foregoing chapters is the fact that Berlin was in all respects inadequately prepared for defense.

Nevertheless, the course of the fighting in Berlin showed that a battle for and in a large city is extremely difficult, not only for the defenders, but even for a far superior attacking force. The experience of Stalingrad, Koenigsberg, and other large cities was confirmed in Berlin.

The following lessons may be drawn from the battle for Berlin.

1. The ability of large cities to defend themselves depends not so much on specially prepared installations, but rather on the extent to which the city is built up. The greater the destruction by fire and explosion in a city, the more suitable it is for defense.

2. The entire planning and directing of the defense should be placed without reservation in the hands of a single, fully responsible commander. All higher agencies not necessary to the city's defense should be evacuated before the fighting begins.

3. Plans should be made well in advance, so that they may be put into effect at the proper time. This applies to the construction of concrete fortifications, the manning of positions, and the administration and distribution of supplies.

4. The defense forces must consist of first-class combat troops. Troops of lesser combat value are not equal to the hard street and house-to-house fighting. These forces should be given instruction in the peculiarities of combat in large cities - commando-type operations, close combat, sniping from

Soviet artillery during the opening phase of the battle for Berlin.

rooftops, and defense against infiltration. There must be sufficient reserves for counterthrusts and the replacement of losses.

5. The following weapons have proved effective: close combat weapons of all types; flak against aerial and ground targets; tank and assault guns for counterthrusts and antitank defense. An ample supply of radio equipment is necessary.

6. It is expedient to evacuate the mass of the population, although a sufficient working force must remain behind to carry on such vital activities as supply, the clearing of rubble, and the operation of workshops and industrial enterprises. This part of the population must be subordinated to the defense commander. Provision should be made to give the population psychological guidance.

7. A strong and efficient military police service is essential.

If the strategic senselessness of the battle for Berlin is disregarded and consideration is given only to the tactical and technical aspect of the operation, the following general conclusion may be reached: In all fields the plans for the defense of Berlin were incoherent and incomplete. The chief reason for this, apart from the total inadequacy of the human and material resources at hand, was the absence of systematic and clear organization, which is a primary requisite in all such planning.

APPENDIX: A SHORT ACCOUNT OF COMBAT OPERATIONS

I. FIGHTING TO THE EAST OF BERLIN
(16 - 22 April 1945)

Before the beginning of the final Russian offensive one panzer division and four panzer grenadier divisions were held in reserve behind the Oder Front. They had suffered severe casualties in the earlier fighting and had not been fully rehabilitated. Two of these units, Panzer Grenadier Divisions "Nordland" and "Nederland," were largely composed of non-German personnel.

In the period from 12 to 15 April the enemy widened the bridgehead on either side of Kuestrin in preparation for the final drive on Berlin. (The major lines of attack are shown in Sketch 2, page 4.) It was already necessary at this early stage to commit Panzer Division "Muencheberg" to action.

On 16 April the enemy opened a large-scale offensive from the Kuestrin bridgehead and from along the Neisse in the Forst - Guben sector against the Fourth Panzer Army of Army Group Schoerner. On the whole the unity or the Oder front was maintained during the first day of attack. Certain units, however, were already so hard pressed that it was necessary to commit another reserve unit, the 25th Panzer Grenadier Division.

On 17 and 18 April the enemy succeeded in making deep inroads into the lines, and the German defenses opposite the bridgehead began to weaken. The moving up of reserves was delayed. On 18 April the 18th Panzer Grenadier Division went into action, followed on 20 April by Panzer Grenadier Division "Nordland" and parts of Panzer Grenadier Division "Nederland." Consequently no effective counterattacks were launched after that time. The LVI Panzer Corps, commanding the forces east of Berlin, could do nothing but delay the Russian advance while engaging in a step-by-step retreat.

The attacking wedge between Forst and Guben pushed forward into open country. The bulk of the forces attacking in this sector turned northward, threatening the flank and rear of the Ninth Army and menacing Berlin from the south. To counter this threat, Division Jahn, a unit still in process of being formed out of Labor Service components, was committed to action by the Army High Command along a forty-kilometer front facing south on either side of Baruth. This was the so-called Armeegruppe Spree. On 20 April the Russians broke through this weak defense line near Baruth, reaching Zossen on 21 April and the southern perimeter of Berlin on 22 April. Some elements of Division Jahn withdrew to Potsdam.

The southern wing of the 1st Russian Army Group, advancing from the Kuestrin bridgehead, swung south against the Erkner - Frankfurt-on-the-Oder line. The center of the army group engaged in heavy fighting with the LVI Panzer Corps, which was pushed back toward Berlin. The northern wing met with little resistance. It reached Werneuchen on 21 April and on the following date advanced by way of Bernau toward the Havel River between Spandau and Oranienburg. When repulsed near Oranienburg, an armored wedge by a bold move crossed the Havel near Henningsdorf, north of Spandau, in the face of weak resistance.

To protect the south flank of the Third Panzer Army, which was still holding out on the lower Oder, Army Group Vistula had previously deployed some security forces, consisting of a few police battalions and Luftwaffe replacement units, along the Finow Canal as far as Oranienburg. On 19 April a naval division had begun moving from Swinemuende to Oranienburg. Owing to the destruction of rail facilities through air attack, only two battalions of this division reached Oranienburg, arriving there just in time to beat back a Russian attempt to cross the Havel. The security forces in the sector from Oranienburg to the upper limits of Eberswalde had been placed under the command of SS Obergruppenfuehrer Steiner.

Since Army Group Vistula did not have at its disposal additional forces to man the sector stretching south of Oranienburg to Spandau, it had requested the Army High Command to provide troops there. At the latter's orders the so-called "Mueller Brigade," scraped together from a few understrength battalions, set out from Doeberitz. Either this force failed to reach the Havel or else it could not put up sufficient resistance; in any case, the Russians succeeded in gaining the west bank of the Havel and thus found themselves in a position to encircle Berlin from the west. On the same day, 22 April, Russian forces approaching from the northeast reached the perimeter of the city near Weissensee and Pankow.

Commentary.

The collapse of the Oder front was an unavoidable consequence of the numerical and material superiority of the Russians. The available reserves were far too weak and even if committed on a mass scale would in the long run have been unable to achieve success. While the bulk of the German forces fought valiantly, the complete failure of the individual units shows that the morale of the German troops was no longer uniformly high. Moreover, it is necessary to take into account not only the shortages in materiel of all kinds and the virtual lack of air power, but the fact that most older units as well as the newly set-up units contained a large number of inexperienced personnel.

Hitler believed that the attack across the Neisse would be aimed at Prague, by way of Dresden. Instead, the main force of the attack was directed at Berlin. In view of this development, Hitler gravely erred in ordering the Ninth Army to stand firm on the central Oder over the protests of Army Group Vistula. The order led to the surrounding of the Ninth Army and the

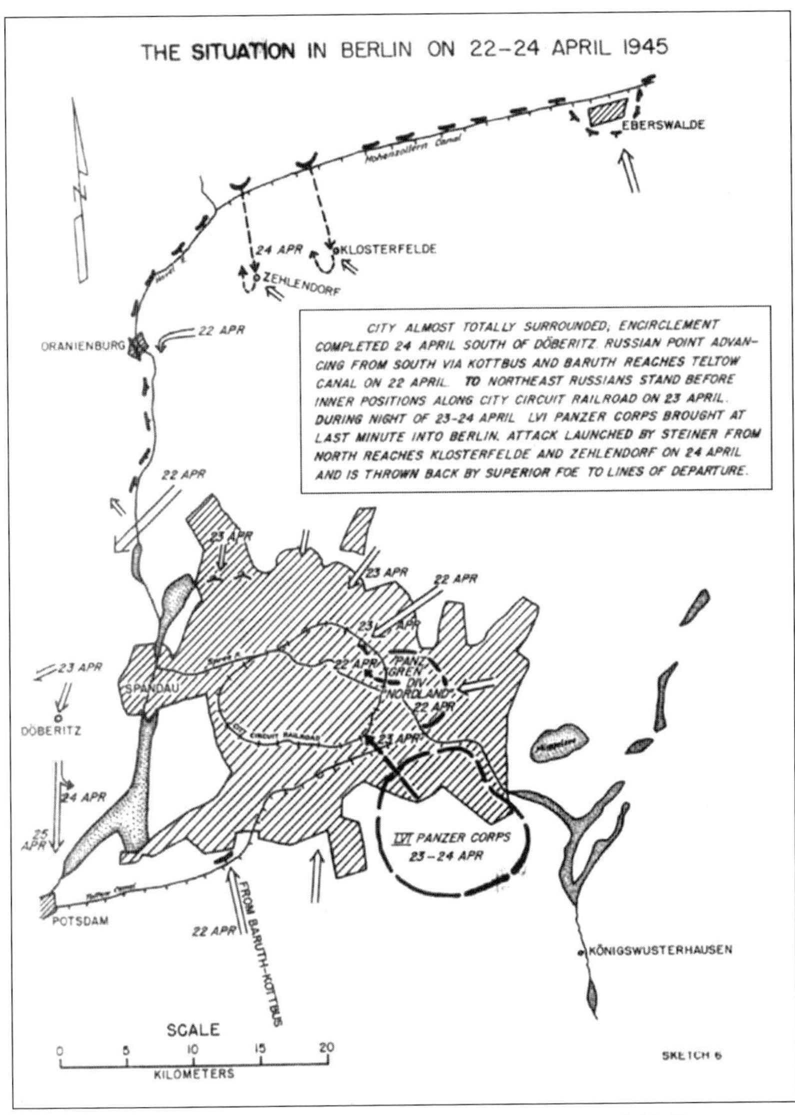

Sketch 6 - The situation in Berlin on 22-24 April 1945

encirclement of Berlin from the south.

The security measures along the Finow Canal proved expedient, but inadequate south of Oranienburg. To assure that troops would occupy this important sector in time, the Army High Command should have made certain that the routes of communication with the west were kept open. But here, as well as on the southern front, the necessary forces were lacking as a further consequence of the Ninth Army's firm stand on the Oder.

The Russian commanders were active in exploiting the gaps effected in the lines to aid the rapid advance of strong motorized and armored forces. They correctly estimated the slight danger threatening the flanks of their spearheads, and armored points advanced boldly north of Spandau. The advance on Berlin itself, however, was cautious and hesitant. Obviously the Russians overestimated the strength of the defense positions and the number of troops occupying them. Army Group Vistula expected that by 21 or 22 April the first Russian tanks would already have reached the Reich Chancellery. Such generals as Rommel or Patton would not have lost this opportunity for a surprise thrust. As long as the LVI Panzer Corps was still east of Berlin, such an attack from the northeast or from the north would have had good chance of success.

Despite the preparations for the defense of Berlin, by 22 April the city was almost helpless against a powerful attack from the south, northeast or north. Along the approximately sixty kilometers of the city perimeter defense ring (not including the western front, which had not yet been attacked), and in the positions along the city circuit railroad, the lines were held almost solely by the Volkssturm and other units of low combat value. The government sector, of course, was still guarded by units of the SS.

II. FIGHTING IN AND AROUND BERLIN (23 - 30 APRIL 1945)

On 23 April the Russians attacked the position along the city perimeter in the south, east, and north, breaking through at several points, and in the east driving forward to the inner defense ring, where they first stopped in the vicinity of the Friedrechshain flak tower.

Advancing by way of Spandau, west of Havel, they reached Doeberitz on 23 April, Nauen on 24 April, and Rathenau on 25

April. Pushing ahead to the south of Doeberitz on 23 April, the enemy had cut off Berlin from the west by evening. Potsdam was also encircled.

On the evening of 23 April, General Weidling took command of the city and that same night moved the troops of the LVI Panzer Corps into Berlin. The divisions were immediately committed at crucial points in the battle lines. Remnants of the 20th Panzer Grenadier Division went into action in the southwest, Panzer Division "Muenchenberg" in the southeast, Panzer Grenadier Division "Nordland" and remnants of Panzer Grenadier Division "Nederland" in the east, and the 18th Panzer Grenadier Division in the northern and southern parts of the Zoo sector. This indication of the distribution of forces can serve only as a general guide, since the position and composition of the units changed daily and even hourly. The Panzer Corps and the SS units under Mohnke now carried the burden of the stiffening resistance to the uninterrupted Russian attacks, which were concentrated in the southeast, east, and north. In the west, Berlin was attacked by comparatively weaker forces, but they were still far superior to the defenders. The forces advancing from the south behind the 1st Ukrainian Army Group had to divert elements against the Ninth Army, Potsdam, and later the Twelfth Army.

In the course of heavy fighting, the German troops were pushed back to the city circuit railroad and even beyond it. By 30 April only the government sector, the immediate vicinity of the Tiergarten and a strip extending westward from the Zoo sector to the Havel River were still held by the defenders. The Russians employed a planned and methodical procedure of attack. Bombing and heavy artillery and mortar fire preceded every fresh assault. The infantry was supported by tanks advancing singly or in group formation and by engineer troops with flame-throwers and demolition equipment. Advances were made by small sectors - street by street and house by house. The

The news of Hitler's death is proclaimed by the Allies.

infantry took every opportunity to infiltrate through back yards, cellar passageways, subway tunnels, and sewers. In this way many of the defense positions were stormed from behind or below.

At first the defenders made use of the prepared positions.

After being driven from these, new vantage points were found in bombed-out lots, cellars, and buildings. The few available tanks sought out suitable firing positions amid the ruins or were used for counterthrusts. Some tanks were dug into position after they ran out of fuel. The defenders fell back for support on the large air-raid bunkers and above all on the flak towers, each of which was tightly enclosed by field fortifications. The artillery had to depend for its firing positions on open squares, parks, and railroad yards. Toward the end of the fighting the remaining guns were closely crowded together in the Tiergarten.

Commentary.

The character of the bitter street fighting and the extensive commitment of materiel on the part of the Russians led to a high expenditure of strength. Thus it was necessary to feed a constant stream of fresh forces into the battle. In contrast to the defenders, the attackers had such forces in large quantity.

The German plans had failed to provide for the timely manning of the city perimeter defense position by adequate numbers of troops. Stronger forces were needed than those finally ordered by the LVI Panzer Corps. After Berlin had been surrounded and the Russians had penetrated into the heart of the city, it would have been impossible, even in the long run, to halt the attackers. Nevertheless, the LVI Panzer Corps possessed sufficient gallantry and fighting strength to inflict heavy losses on the Russians and to resist for more than a week behind steadily contracting lines.

After the Russians had failed to take the city in the first onslaught before the arrival of the Panzer Corps, the systematic combat procedure adopted by them became expedient.

III. THE RELIEF ATTACKS (24 - 29 April 1945)

1. From the North.

As soon as a Russian break-through toward Bernau by way of Wriezen appeared imminent, Army Group Vistula became

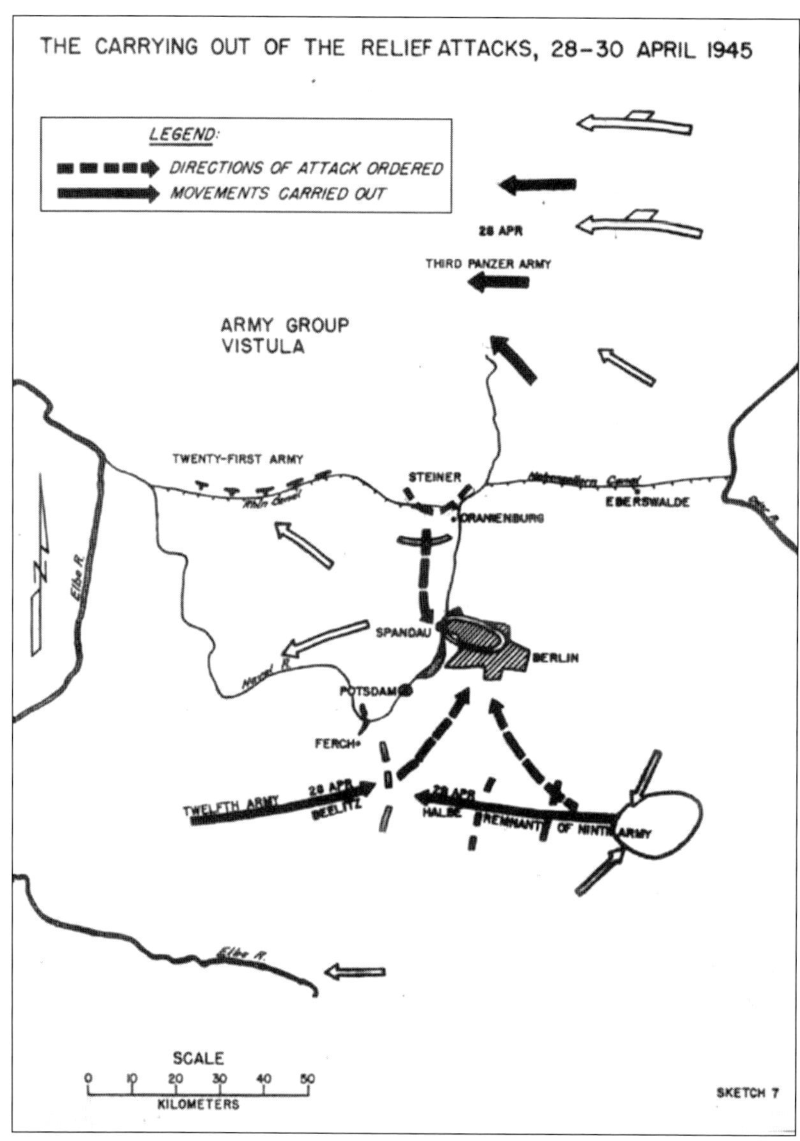

Sketch 7 - The Carrying Out of Relief Attacks, 28-30 April 1945

justifiably concerned over the Third Panzer Army's southern flank. Measures taken for the protection of the canal line from Eberswalde to Oranienburg have been pointed out above. When the Russians succeeded in crossing the Havel River on 22 April, the possibility of a drive in the direction of Mecklenburg or Hamburg presented an ever greater danger for the rear of the army group. The only possibility for countering this threat was to launch a local attack southward from the Finow Canal against the deep flank of the Russian spearhead. That same day, 22 April, the army group ordered SS Obergruppenfuehrer Steiner to direct such an attack, and for this purpose placed at his disposal about seven improvised battalions. This mixed task force was not ready for action until the morning of 24 April. The attack caught some Russian security detachments by surprise and pushed forward without interruption for about ten kilometers to Zehlendorf and Klosterfelde. The Russians then threw stronger forces into action and drove the attackers across the Finow Canal and back to their lines of departure.

The attack had fulfilled its purpose by diverting the attention of Russian forces which would otherwise have driven further westward. The same purpose was accomplished by holding a bridgehead at Eberswalde, which was attacked for days by the Second Polish Army. Hitler, however, saw in the operation a chance to relieve Berlin by launching an attack with stronger forces from the north, whereupon he ordered SS Obergruppenfuehrer Steiner to direct a strong attack on Spandau from the area west of Oranienburg. Keitel laid repeated stress on these orders by appearing personally at army group headquarters. For this operation, troops were to be brought in from the Elbe. The 28th Panzer Grenadier Division, which had been fighting near Eberswalde, was also to participate. In the meantime the situation had radically changed. In the Oranienburg sector SS Obergruppenfuehrer Steiner, with only one hastily assembled division still at his disposal, stood face to face with the Russians. On 25 April the lines of the Third Panzer Army had been pierced south of Stettin by a major attack, and it was necessary for the army to withdraw to the west while at the same time abandoning the Finow Canal. The 25th Panzer Grenadier Division was urgently needed to support the Third Panzer Army and thus make possible the latter's withdrawal, and

Clutching panzer fausts the Volkssturm march boldly forth into combat.

it was in fact committed by the army group to this front. Corps Holste, coming up from the Elbe, had to move in with utmost speed in order to lengthen the deep southern flank of the army group along the Rhin Canal and there halt a Russian attack directed toward Hamburg.

A sharp clash now developed between the commander of Army Group Vistula and General Keitel. General Keitel regarded as treason General Heinrici's efforts to save at least the remaining elements of his army group. On 29 April he relieved Henrici of his post and appointed Generaloberst Student as his successor; Generaloberst von Tippelskirch assumed command until the new commander's arrival. This shift effected no change in the actual situation, however. The movements ordered by Generaloberst Heinrici were carried out, and the bulk of the Third Panzer Army, the Steiner forces, and the troops grouped under the Twenty-first Army along the Rhin River surrendered to the Western Allies.

2. From the Southeast.

The Ninth Army, in compliance with strict orders from Hitler, had remained so long on the central Oder that it was encircled by the enemy. Hitler gave orders on 23 April that the Ninth Army was to break out in the direction of Mariendorf, on the southern perimeter of Berlin, to join forces with the Twelfth Army for a relief attack on the capital. This order presupposed on the part of the Ninth Army a freedom of action which it no longer possessed. Shortly before receiving the order, the commander, General der Infanterie Busse, had decided to attempt a breakthrough to the west by way of Halbe in order to continue in the same direction under cover of the extensive forests in that area. The army adhered to this decision even after the receipt of Hitler's orders. After bitter fighting, the Ninth Army, with a force of 30,000 men, succeeded in breaking through the Russian encirclement and meeting the Twelfth Army near Beelitz on 29 - 30 April.

3. From the West.

The Twelfth Army, under the command of General der Panzer Truppen Wenck, was originally assigned to the Magdeburg area, with its front facing west. On 23 April it received orders to face about and, leaving only the weakest security detachments on the Elbe, to attack Berlin and liberate the capital with the assistance of the Ninth Army. The army succeeded in quickly regrouping its forces and, with the three divisions of the XX Corps protecting its flanks, reached the Beelitz - Ferch sector on 28 April. There it was joined by escaped elements of those troops which had withdrawn to Potsdam under General Reymann and by the remains of the Ninth Army.

After that the Twelfth Army barely had time to return to the Elbe, where it was captured by the Americans. At no time was there any possibility of continuing the attack on Berlin.

Commentary.

The orders given for the contemplated relief attacks failed completely to take into account the actual conditions in the field. They nevertheless greatly stimulated the hope and will to resist on the part of the defenders. After the Twelfth Army failed in its

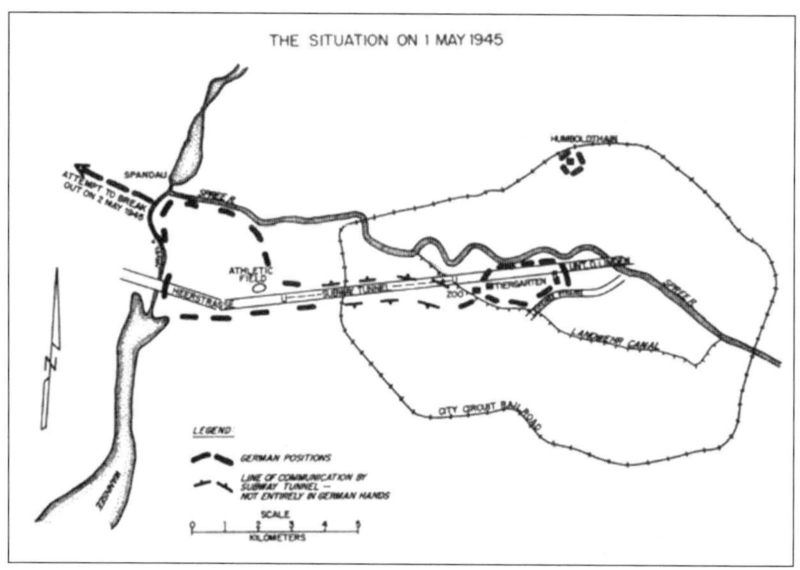

Sketch 8 - the situation on 1 May 1945

attempted attack, Hitler committed suicide.

With the death of Hitler, the commanders outside Berlin found themselves in a position to make clear decisions of their own with a view to saving their troops. Keitel's senseless orders were no longer heeded.

IV. ENGAGEMENTS IN BERLIN AFTER 30 APRIL AND THE FINAL SURRENDER

On 30 April, soon after Hitler's death, General Weidling received a letter prepared at 1300 hours that same day and signed by Hitler. It left the defenders free to attempt to break out of the city, but at the same time forbade them to surrender. Since Weidling did not regard a break-through on a mass scale as feasible, he allowed the troops under his command to leave the city on their own initiative. This order was issued by Weidling from the Reichs Chancellery, which he was unable to leave since 29 April. Shortly afterwards, Goebbels intervened and in his capacity as minister forbade all attempts to leave the city, announcing at the same time, that he would enter into negotiations with the Russians. Since Weidling naturally supposed that these negotiations would lead to a cease fire, he revoked his earlier order on the afternoon of 30 April.

On 1 May, it became evident that Goebbel's negotiations were not leading to a capitulation, Weidling hesitated between attempting a break-through and surrendering. On the afternoon of 1 May the troops received a new order, stating that a break-through would be attempted that evening. In the meantime, however, Weidling had decided to capitulate. He also revoked his second break-through order and on the evening of 1 May called the commanders who could still be reached to the Bendler Bunker and informed them of his intention to surrender the next morning. The offer was communicated to the Russians by radio and by Colonel (GSC) von Duffing as truce representative. An offer of surrender made independently of Weidling's by State Secretary Fritsche - each being unaware of the other's action - came to nought. Goebbels, after the failure of his attempted negotiations, by which he hoped to be recognized as minister in a new government, had again proclaimed a fight to the bitter end. He then committed suicide.

The vacillation of the leaders, the orders and counterorders, had produced great confusion among the troops. Many combat groups had not received the order calling off the break-through, while others had received no orders at all. Many units, in small or large groups, moved out from the Zoo sector by way of the subway tunnel, past the radio tower and Ruhleben, to the Havel. A break-through across the northern bridge at Spandau was made by a force with tank support, although heavy losses resulted. Individual detachments and stragglers succeeded in escaping, but the bulk of these forces were encircled in the open terrain north of Nauen and taken prisoner.

The surrender was effected in Berlin on the morning of 2 May, although not without difficulty. In many instances officers announcing the capitulation were accused of treason and threatened with death. Individual combat groups, especially

The Volkssturm had little chance of making an impression on the advancing Soviets.

among the SS, refused to surrender and fought on for hours, and even days, to the last man. The bulk of the defenders fell prisoner to the Russians on 2 May.

Commentary.

To continue the defense was hopeless and could only have led to further senseless losses among the troops and the civilian population. Likewise, attempts by entire units to break out of the city in a body had not the slightest chance of success. That this was tried in many instances only shows how great was the fear of capture by the Russians.

WHAT THE GERMANS LEARNED AT WARSAW

Intelligence Bulletin, April 1945

The Germans gained so much experience in street fighting while suppressing the first general uprising of armed Polish forces in Warsaw that the official German "Notes for Panzer Troops" takes cognizance of the lessons learned during these operations. Employing the popular German Army training method of listing incorrect and correct procedures in parallel columns, "Notes for Panzer Troops" sets forth a number of German errors in the Warsaw fighting, and supplies official comment on the methods which should have been employed in each case.

The observations in the "right" column take on an added significance, in view of a statement by the Inspector General of Panzer Troops to the effect that the underlying principles must be applied in all street fighting.

WRONG	RIGHT
A large number of heavy support weapons (assault guns, heavy howitzers, assault howitzers, self-propelled antitank guns, and infantry heavy weapons) were used in an uncoordinated fashion, with a consequent lack of effect. The fire of the support weapons was not used for immediate pushing forward.	All available support weapons, including artillery and aircraft, are concentrated on approved targets. During the concentration the infantry prepares to attack as soon as the last shell has fallen. Armored vehicles accompanying the infantry, to keep down any hostile soldiers who are still alive and who try to reappear.
Our troops mainly used streets. (In street fighting the enemy can take advantage of innumerable hiding places. Absence of visible enemy therefore by no means implies actual absence of enemy.)	Walls of adjoining houses are blasted, and troops move forward through the houses. Mopping-up parties of infantry follow. (Making such covered approaches facilitates evacuation of wounded and supply of ammunition and rations.)

WRONG	RIGHT
Houses or blocks were not consolidated immediately after capture. Infantry lingered around the entrances, doing nothing.	As soon as a building has been taken, it is consolidated; windows and other openings are turned into firing ports. Since underground passages and sewers provide the enemy with cover and means of communication, the entrances to cellars, stairs, and so on are to be given special attention. If subterranean passages cannot be mopped up immediately, the entrances must be barricaded, or blown in and guarded. Troops will not stand around idly.
Completely ruined houses were regarded as being no longer of use to the enemy. (It was found, however, that the enemy made considerable use of completely destroyed buildings.)	Even the most completely ruined houses must be occupied or covered by fire. Roving patrols are detailed to deny access to them and to ferret out any hostile stragglers who may have occupied them.
Many of the houses that we occupied had been almost completely destroyed by our own fire, thus denying our attacking troops positions and cover.	As far as possible, random destruction of potential cover can be prevented by strict discipline. Only outbuildings affording the enemy covered approach to vital points should be destroyed.
Armored vehicles were used to knock down barricades and walls, to push aside abandoned vehicles and guns, and to perform other tasks for which they are not suited.	The fire power of the armored vehicles must be conserved by all means. In street fighting they are very much exposed to close-range antitank weapons. This makes them fundamentally unsuited for "bulldozer" tasks. The accompanying infantry therefore protects them against surprise attack of any kind. When attacking barricades and obstacles, the infantry approaches first and forces passage through the obstacles. Squads of civilians later are put to work to complete the clearing of debris.

WRONG	RIGHT
Our troops failed to make sufficient use of their rifles. The enemy was not sufficiently harassed.	Rifle and machine-gun fire must be delivered promptly and steadily from all newly captured buildings. Rifle fire is concentrated on group targets to keep the enemy's heads down. The enemy is not given a moment's rest, but feels himself perpetually observed and engaged. Rapid opening of fire is especially important, to avoid giving the enemy time to withdraw to alternate positions.
The supposedly non-combatant and "harmless" population was not kept under observation, and seldom was employed to clear debris.	All able-bodied civilians are employed to clear debris. The German Army must enforce this point relentlessly, even when the work is performed under fire. (In this case the whole population was more or less directly assisting the insurgent Polish troops.)
Sufficient cunning was not employed to counter the enemy's tactics.	Tricks must be employed to draw fire and silence it. Our methods must change constantly; feints and other tricks and imaginative tactics must be devised.
The liaison between the various assault detachments was generally too loose, and signal communications were inadequately used. Radio and telephone conversations were practically always in the clear.	Assault detachments are instructed in methods of cooperation, use of fire, and movement. Cooperation will be improved if the assault detachments are kept constantly in the picture and if they report regularly on their position and intentions.

The Inspector General of Panzer Troops adds a final comment of his own. He says, "When tanks are used in street fighting, they should be employed like the so-called 'tank-Infantry teams' used in Normandy—that is, small infantry units will be detailed to cooperate directly with tanks. The tougher the fighting, the greater our casualties will be if the following principles are not observed: (1) no splitting of forces, (2) thorough and purposeful concentration of fire, (3) immediate infantry exploitation of tank fire and (4) the closest mutual support throughout each action.

THE GERMAN VOLKSSTURM

Intelligence Bulletin, February 1945

Of the measures taken to mobilize speedily the last manpower resources of the German nation, the most extreme is the creation of the Volkssturm, a national militia designed to supplement the defense of the homeland. The call to arms, which was issued on 18 October 1944, was literally a dragnet, sweeping into a single organization virtually all German males between the ages of 16 and 60 who were not already members of the German Armed Forces. The creation of the Volkssturm serves a double purpose, as far as the Nazi Party is concerned: first, to strengthen the defense of the Reich, and, second, to keep a large part of the population so thoroughly under military control that any incipient revolt against the Party will have a hard time thriving. It is the enemy's intention to have a strong hard core of Nazi fanatics dominating the Volkssturm at all levels.

In announcing the formation of the new militia, Hitler designated the Chief of the Storm Troopers, Schepmann, as Inspector of Weapons Training, and the Chief of the Nazi Motor Corps, Kraus, as Inspector of Technical Training. Himmler is charged with ordering the actual employment of the Volkssturm for local defense. However, it must be remembered that the militia is currently in the training stage, with its members continuing their ordinary jobs. When the Volkssturm is operating on a full-time basis, its employment may be directed by the Army.

The Volkssturm is definitely a bottom-of-the-barrel organization. Although it may succeed in mustering more than ten million men for local defense inside the Reich, a conservative estimate indicates that less than half of these will be physically fit.

Whether dressed in civilian clothes or varied uniforms, Volkssturm members wear the organization's arm band.

In one capacity or another, many of the Volkssturm personnel already were contributing their services to the German war effort when the call to arms was issued. It will be recalled that dozens of Nazi semi-military, service, and political organizations, regimenting practically every walk of German life, had been in existence for some time. Because of these organizations, and because Nazi Party officialdom itself is so extensive that it even includes city "block leaders", the Nazi authorities long had had a very fair knowledge of the military and service possibilities of every male in Germans. Much had been done to exploit German manpower on a part-time basis wherever full-time service could not be performed. Thus service in the Volkssturm becomes merely an added duty for men who already have part-time jobs in other defense organizations or who work in war industries. As the Germans envisage it, a man who performs ARP tasks during an air raid, who has a route to patrol as a member of the Stadtwacht (City Guard), or who is a skilled laborer in a Messerschmidt plant will take his post in a Volkssturm squad and fight as an infantryman when his home area is attacked by Allied ground forces.

It is logical to infer that, as Volkssturm units are being formed, the abilities, physical fitness, and war work of the recruits will be taken into account. Limited-service personnel will be given local or static defense missions. Invalids and cripples, it is reported, will be reserved for headquarters work. Although youths of 16 are to be included in the Volkssturm, the lower age brackets in general are likely not to be represented very generously, in view of the fact that the German Armed Forces increasingly are drafting men younger than 18. Also, if a Volkssturmmann is drafted into the Armed Forces, his membership in the militia automatically terminates.

Despite the fact that the Volkssturm is inducting by age classes, an appeal for "volunteers" is being conducted in the usual Nazi manner. Working through the factory cells of the German Labor Front organization and other groups directly supervised by the Party, Nazi leaders have induced the entire personnel of certain factories and businesses to "volunteer" in a body, with the result that recruits pour in as fast as the training facilities can handle them, and faster than if they all had been drafted formally.

With the Nazi Party in charge of organizing the Volkssturm, the early stages in the development of this national militia have been expedited. Although each Gauleiter, or Nazi District Leader, is charged with the leadership, enrollment, and organization of the Volkssturm in his district, the largest Volkssturm unit seems to correspond to the next smaller territorial subdivision of the Nazi Party organization—the Kreis. In a city, Volkssturm organization might run something like this:

Territorial Political Unit

Kreis (roughly equivalent to a U.S. county; there are 920 kreise in Greater Germany)
Military Unit: Bataillon (battalion)

Territorial Political Unit

Ortsgruppe (roughly equivalent to a U.S. Congressional district)
Military Unit: Kompanie (company)

Territorial Political Unit

Zelle (literally "a cell"; roughly equivalent to a U.S. precinct)
Military Unit: Zug (platoon)

Territorial Political Unit

Block (a city block)
Military Unit: Gruppe (squad)

Not only each Gauleiter, but each Kreisleiter, has a Volkssturm Chief of Staff to assist in handling militia problems.

Although differentials may be introduced in the selection and assignment of personnel, Nazi leaders assert that all Volkssturm members will be given the same instruction. This is to consist of infantry training, with special emphasis on close combat. The rifle is the basic weapon. It is to be supplemented by submachine guns and light machine guns. Since there is almost no limit to the number of models of such weapons taken over by the Germans from conquered nations, it would be difficult to state exactly which small-arms models the Volkssturm will use.

German males between the age of 16 and 60 are liable for service in the new national militia.

German, Czech, and Polish Mauser rifles already are in service, and use will be made of the many thousands of captured Russian rifles and machine guns. Other equipment includes egg hand grenades and potato-masher hand grenades. For antitank defense, the Panzerfaust hollow-charge launchers have been promised to the Volkssturm. (The latest of these recoilless weapons has a range of 88 yards; earlier models have a range of only 33 yards.) German bazookas also may be furnished. Instruction in the handling of antitank and antipersonnel mines already is being given.

At present any turnout of the Volkssturm is likely to present a rag-tag-and-bobtail appearance, in dress as well as armament. The only item of clothing or insignia currently issued is a black

The rifle is the basic weapon of the Volkssturm, which receives infantry training, with special emphasis on close combat.

arm band with the lettering "Deutscher Volkssturm" in a light color and with the word "Wehrmacht" directly underneath this. The Nazis have asserted that this arm band officially makes the Volkssturm members a part of the Wehrmacht (Armed Forces). It is left to the individual to provide the rest of the clothing. Uniforms of the Storm Troopers, Hitler Youth, and Party territorial leaders will be encountered. Many men will simply wear civilian clothes. Already the lack of complete official uniform has caused a great deal of disgruntlement throughout the new militia. Many members feel that they are assuming the duties of soldiers, with none of the privileges. (Incidentally, there is no remuneration for service in Volkssturm, except when a member is taking part in actual combat.)

The effectiveness of the Volkssturm remains to be tested. In the past, organized defense of urban and rural areas by the local populace fighting in support of regular troops has indicated that a people defending their homes under such conditions are capable of putting up a most determined defense. Volkssturm elements were used in combat near Metz, but the poor showing that they made must be attributed primarily to the fact that they had only recently been mustered and that most of their brief time in the militia had been spent in digging fortifications. In future months the Nazis will discover and try to correct the outstanding defects of the Volkssturm, and their unquestioned talent for organization and military training must be expected to show at least a few tangible results. Just how much success the Nazis will have in using Volkssturm members as guerrilla fighters after local areas have been overrun by the Allies cannot be predicted. Much would seem to depend on how hard a core of Nazi fanatics each element contains.

*[**Note:** As the Intelligence Bulletin goes to press, it is reported that rank insignia worn by the Volkssturm consist of silver stars worn on the lapel or on the collar. One star will indicate a squad leader, two a platoon leader, three a company commander, and four a battalion commander.]*

THE PANZERHANDMINE 3 A MAGNETIC HOLLOW CHARGE

Intelligence Bulletin, May 1945

The Panzerhandmine 3 (which the Germans abbreviate to P.H.M. 3) is a magnetic hollow charge intended for use as a close-combat weapon against Allied tanks and similar armored targets. A series of magnets around the bottom of the charge cause the weapon to adhere to the target. The charge is German Air Force issue, and is the Air Force counterpart of the standard German Army magnetic hollow charge 3 kg. (Hafthohlladung 3 Kg.), which it resembles in design and employment.

German documents state that the Panzerhandmine 3 will penetrate 6-inch armor plate, creating a 1 1/4-inch hole and causing a great deal of scaling within the vehicle. Outside the vehicle, metal splinters may be expected to be hurled as far away

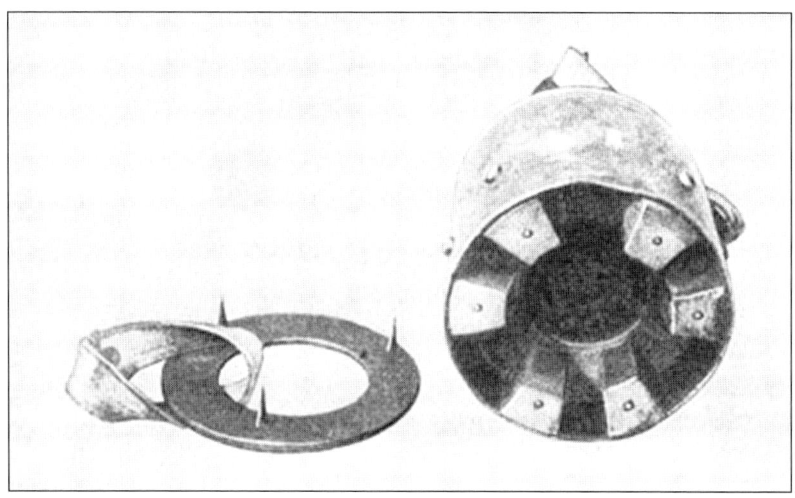

A bottom view of the Panzerhandmine 3. Note the six magnets for use against metal surfaces, and the keeper with spikes for use against wooden surfaces.

The Panzerhandmine 3, a magnetic hollow charge.

as 100 yards.

This hollow-charge weapon is 10 3/4 inches high and 5 1/2 inches in diameter, and weighs 8 pounds. It contains a 2 1/2-

pound charge of TNT or RDX/TNT. A compressed-paper body encases the charge and the magnets. A web carrying handle is attached to a metal neck band. The hemispherical cavity of the hollow charge is closed with a metal sheet liner.

Three pairs of magnets are mounted around the interior of the compressed-paper skirt. In transit these magnets are protected by an iron keeper ring, which has a web handle fastened to it for easy withdrawal. On one side of the keeper are three equidistant spikes, which permit the charge to be attached to wooden surfaces. The keeper is reversed in transit, so that the spikes fit between the magnets.

The Panzerhandmine 3 is fired with a yellow-head, 7 1/2-second-delay friction igniter.

CONCRETE STICK HAND GRENADE

Intelligence Bulletin, June 1945

Large quantities of German concrete stick, or "potato masher", grenades have been recovered in various areas of the European Theater. Although it formerly had been supposed that such grenades were local improvisations, evidence now suggests that their design has been accorded official recognition. Two types have been found.

Type 1 consists of a wooden handle, rectangular in cross-section, with a 3/8-inch-square groove running the length of the handle. A length of cord, attached to a pull fuze, operates through this groove. Often the other end of the cord is tied to a small piece of wood, which serves as a pull knob. This is wired to the end of the handle with soft, easily broken shear wire.

The forward end of the wooden handle is slotted to form two prongs similar to those of a tuning fork. Iron wire is wrapped

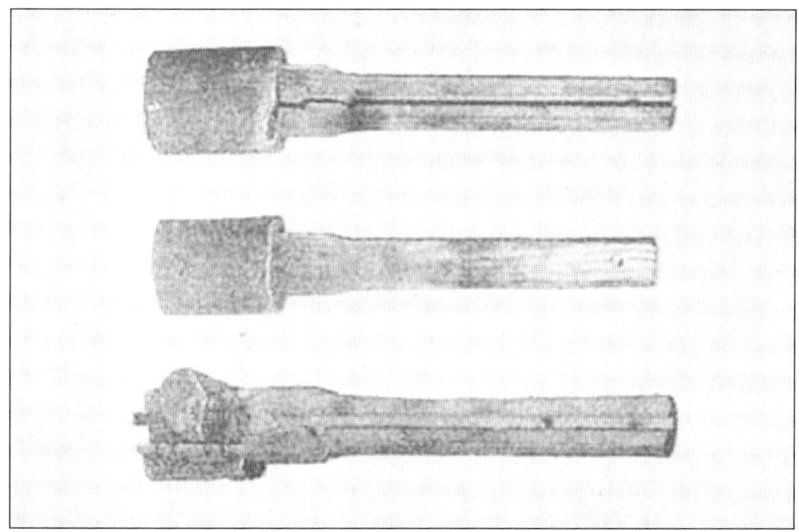

German concrete stick hand grenade, Type 1, with stick TNT inserted in the cavity.

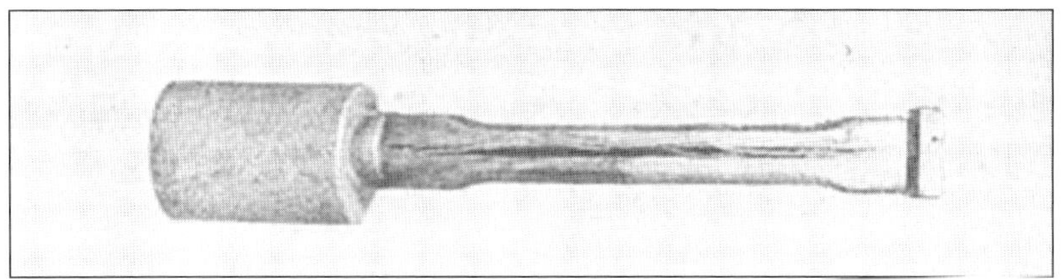

German concrete stick hand grenade, Type 2, with stick TNT embedded in the concrete.

around these prongs, partly to strengthen the concrete, but chiefly to secure the concrete head to the handle. The head has a hollow core to accommodate a standard stick TNT demolition charge 1 1/4 inches in diameter. Two metal inserts above the wooden prongs reinforce the cavity, and permit the insertion of the standard stick charge.

At the base of the concrete head is a small square of translucent waterproof paper over a cardboard square of equal size. There is a hole 3/4-inch in diameter in the center of the card-board, to admit the igniter to the bursting charge. This hole is aligned with the square groove in the handle.

Type 2 resembles Type 1, but is much simpler. Instead of a hollow in the head of the wooden handle to hold the stick charge, a semicircular cavity is milled into the wood, the explosive charge is placed in this cavity, and the whole assembly then is centered in the concrete mold. It will be noted that in the case of Type 2 the charge is actually molded into the concrete, and projects about 3/8 inch on the end toward the handle.

In both types the explosive charge is the stick TNT demolition charge, Bohrpatrone 28, containing about 3 1/2 ounces of explosive and coated with waxed paper. The stick is 4 inches long, slightly more than an inch in diameter, and has a threaded aluminum insert cast into the explosive to accommodate standard German detonators. The usual detonator well is cast into the stick, and the cavity is sealed with a red sticker, which denotes the presence of TNT. The standard B.Z. 24 friction pull fuze, having a delay element of 4 to 5 seconds, is used.

GERMAN POSITION WARFARE REVERTS TO TRENCH LINES IN THE EAST

Tactical and Technical Trends,
No. 51, October 1944

German defensive tactics in position warfare, hitherto subordinated to offensive principles in modern German military thought, have undergone considerable change on the Eastern front under the stress of a shortage of manpower. the mounting pressure of United Nations offensives, and superior Soviet mobility and massed artillery fire.

The familiar German hedgehog systems of mutually supporting strongpoints have been replaced on the long Soviet front with extensive field fortifications laid out in continuous lines. These lines of trenches, reminiscent of World War I, are reinforced with barrier systems of wire, ditches, and mines for protection against infantry and tanks. Deep shelters are integrated in the trench systems to provide cover for personnel and matériel. Dense networks of fire from automatic weapons and infantry mortars cover the field works. The fire plans of these weapons are coordinated with local counterattacks of small units and the direct fire of mobile antitank guns and infantry howitzers, employed singly or in small groups.

Success of the hedgehog system depended upon adequate reserves and sufficient mobility and firepower to launch decisive counterattacks. In Russia, these hedgehogs were based on fortified centers, usually a town or village, and included mutually supporting strong points, intermediate areas under light control, and strong patrols of tanks, self-propelled guns, and motorized infantry (see fig. 1).

German manpower difficulties, coupled with superior Soviet

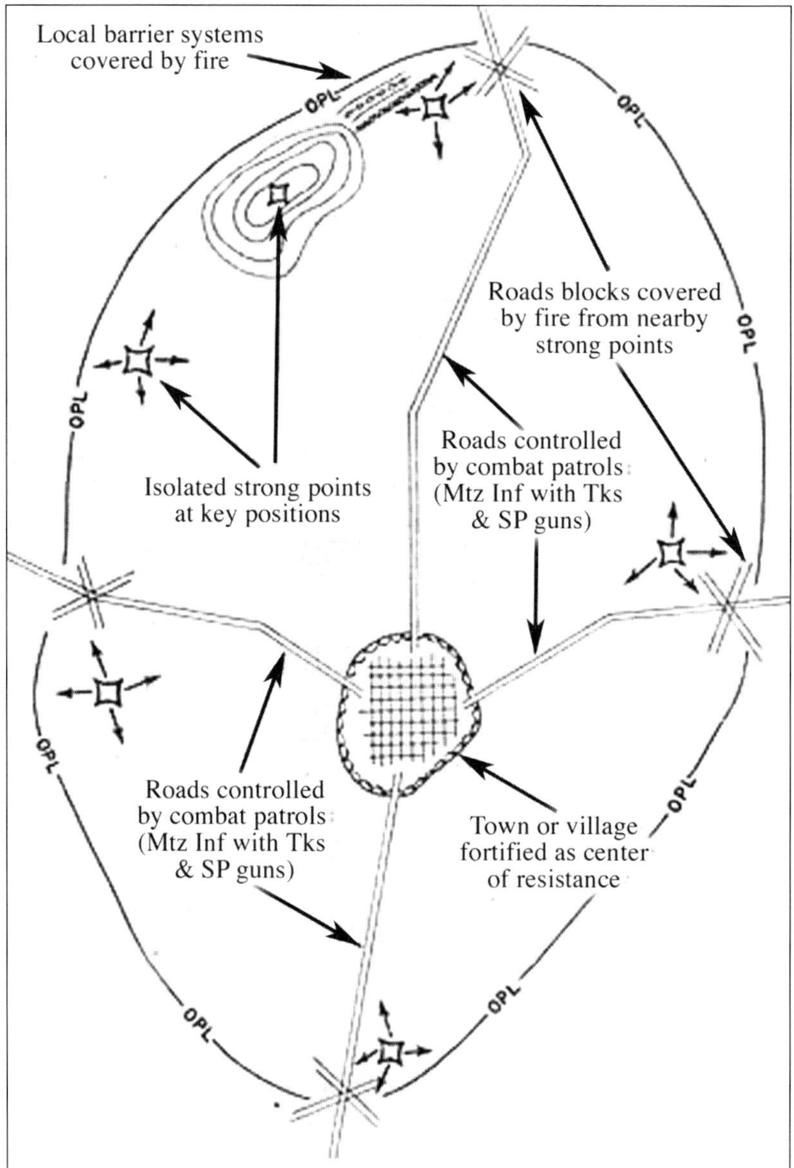

Figure 1. Typical German hedgehog used in elastic defense system.

mobility and firepower, brought about the radical change in German defensive tactics, and in 1943 there began a trend that has developed into a defense based on lines of trenches. Difficulties experienced by the Germans in the transition to linear defenses have been reflected recently in the sharp criticism by German commanders of defense methods and of individual and unit training of German forces on the Eastern front.

SOVIETS STRESS MOBILITY

The Soviets coped effectively with the hedgehogs and with the defensive tactics employed with such a system, by achieving extreme mobility with both infantry and cavalry, not only in winter but also in other seasons. Effective strategic and tactical massing, especially of artillery, was correlated with the movements of mobile forces. Furthermore, Soviet designers developed highly maneuverable tanks that were "good mudders", so that Russian armored forces were a threat at times when German armor bogged down. The Germans, excessively roadbound on the Russian terrain, could match the Soviet forces neither in mobility nor in massed firepower. The result was that, with the hedgehog system of defense, German mobile reserves were seriously hampered in their mission of supporting threatened centers of resistance and strong points by the interdiction fire of massed artillery and by swift penetrations of mobile forces.

According to recent Soviet analyses of German tactics in Krasnaya Zvezda (Red Star). official newspaper of the Soviet Army, the aim of the German High Command is now to construct linear defenses of comparatively shallow depth and compactness to cover the entire length of the Soviet-German front.

Although the Germans still show adaptability in their use of the means of positional warfare, an ability to learn from the methods of their opponents. and aggressiveness in counterattack, their present defense system is an admission of inferior means, lesser mobility, lesser fire power, and loss of air supremacy. Their defense has become one of delaying action and attrition rather than bold, decisive action, and in many ways is a reversion to the positional warfare of World War I.

STRUCTURE OF DEFENSE SYSTEMS

German General of Artillery Sinnhuber reviewed the 1943 campaign in a memorandum "Our Fundamental Weaknesses in Dealing with Russian Tactics" in which he attributed German defeats chiefly to the absence of strongly fortified defensive positions capable of withstanding Soviet artillery and tanks. He recommendeded—

1. Shortening defensive sectors of the principal fronts with the view of building a more compact system of defense, particularly in depth.
2. Building modern defenses, using as much concrete and timber as possible.
3. Using more mechanized equipment to replace men.
4. Achieving artillery supremacy.

Current German defenses rely primarily on trenches and continuous antitank obstacles, in combination with strong points and centers of resistance. This system of defense, according to the German High Command, makes it possible to economize in manpower and to reduce casualties from artillery and mortars. It also aids in concealing the movement of men and light infantry equipment. (See fig. 2.)

The Germans believe, however, that trench defenses have many imperfections, the principal one being their vulnerability to flank attacks after a wedge has been driven into the line by enemy forces.

Last year the German High Command issued a "Manual for the Construction of Positions on the Eastern Front" in which the continuous trench is taken as the basis of defense construction. The manual provides for the building of continuous trenches in the forward edge and along the main line of resistance, to a depth of 1 to 2 miles, connected with a series of strong points located in the forward edge and with resistance centers placed in depth. (See fig. 2.) The Germans follow this scheme as a model, altering it to fit special conditions of terrain and other

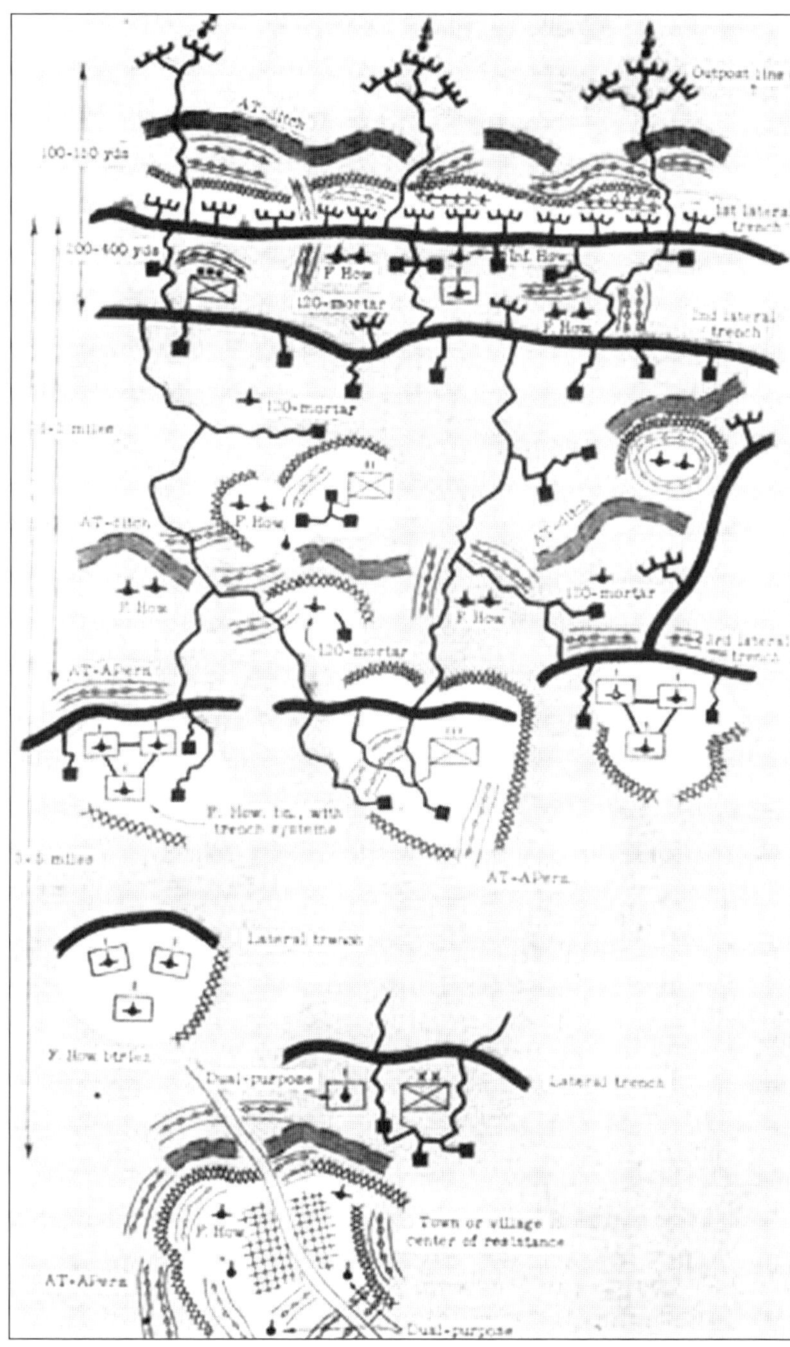

Figure 2. Continuous trenches used as a basis of German defense, with strong points and resistance centers disposed in depth.

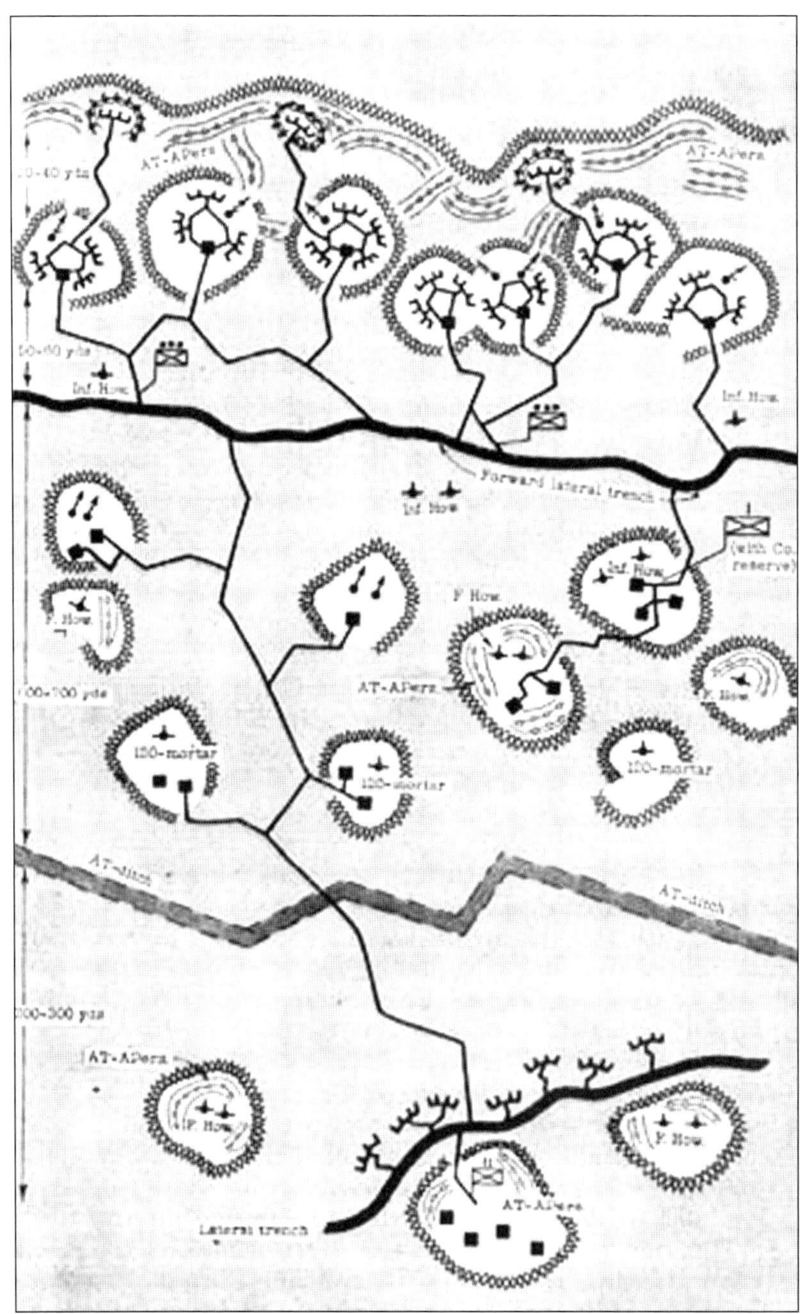

Figure 3. Where continuous-trench systems are not possible, the Germans place strong points in the forward edge of the position.

circumstances.

In important sectors the Germans have built a compact, many-echeloned, continuous defense system. The central defensive zone usually has seven or more lines of continuous trenches. Rear areas also have continuous defenses with a large number of trenches and communication passages. Steel and concrete structures reinforce sectors considered especially critical. Secondary front sectors are defended by scattered centers of resistance and strong points.

CONNECTING TRENCH NETWORK

As a rule, all the engineering structures within a defense area are connected by a dense network of trenches and communication passages. Quite often the Germans build antitank ditches in connection with resistance centers and strong points. These antitank ditches are constructed both in front of the first line of defense and in depth. At important sectors of defense the antitank ditches are dug in three or four rows.

During offensive operations in the spring of 1944, in the Crimea and other sectors, the Red Army encountered a new type of defense construction—a combination of strung points in the forward edge, trenches, and antitank ditches disposed in depth. (See fig. 3.) The Germans employ this defense scheme when conditions do not permit construction of a series of continuous trenches, and when it is possible to build antitank ditches in the forward edge.

The strong points are built for one infantry squad and consist of dugouts, fire trenches, and machine-gun platforms. They are surrounded by barbed-wire entanglements, and are so constructed that they can defend themselves from all sides. In front of these, strong points, at a distance of 30 to 40 yards, the Germans erect two or three unbroken rows of barbed-wire entanglements with concertinas. Within the entanglements are individual firing pits, occupied at night by double sentry posts.

Antitank and antipersonnel mine fields fill the area between the entanglements and the squad strong points.

About 50 to 60 yards to the rear of the squad strong points there is a continuous lateral trench, 6 feet deep and 2 1/2 feet wide, connected with the strong points by communication trenches. Six or seven hundred yards to the rear of this forward lateral trench is a continuous antitank ditch behind which, at a distance of 200 to 300 yards, are switch positions for battalion reserves.

In especially critical sectors the Germans build a special type of trench. It is about 6 feet wide and from 7 to 10 feet deep. The walls are almost perpendicular and are constructed in unusually straight and long sections, about 100 yards or longer. At every angle in the trench a concealed machine-gun nest is constructed, making it possible to direct fire lengthwise along the straight trench sector.

TRENCH FOR QUICK SHIFT

The forward lateral trench is carefully camouflaged to make it invisible to ground and air reconnaissance. Its principal use is to make possible the shifting of men and equipment along the forward edge of defense. In case the Soviets gain possession of a strong point, the Germans who survive the attack move into the trench where they join the reserves and continue their resistance.

Light machine guns and antitank rifles are emplaced in the squad strong points; heavy machine gums are at emplacements at a distance of about 150 to 200 yards behind the continuous trench. The latter direct fire toward the intervals between strong points and over the heads of their own troops.

Mortars are placed 400 to 500 yards behind the continuous trench, usually on reverse slopes. Antitank guns are 200 to 400 yards from the forward edge. Heavy antitank guns, infantry howitzers, and supporting artillery are placed behind the antitank ditch at about 800 to 1,000 yards from the forward lateral trench.

Command posts of platoon leaders are, as a rule, along the line of the continuous trench; company command posts are 200 to 300 yards behind the continuous trench; battalion command posts are in the zone of switch positions from battalion reserves. Both command posts and firing positions of antitank guns, heavy infantry weapons, and artillery are so constructed that they can defend themselves from all sides. They are also connected with the continuous trench.

Command posts of regiments and divisions, regimental and division reserves, and division artillery have the same positions as in the ordinary continuous system of defense shown in figure 2.

To decrease their losses from Soviet artillery, mortars, and tanks, the Germans prefer to build their defenses on reverse slopes, construction and layout being essentially the same as previously outlined. However, the outpost line and advance artillery observation points are placed on the forward slope facing the attacking forces. The outpost line is in most cases constructed as a false line. (See the following section on "The False First Line".) The real outpost line is located on the reverse slope about 300 to 400 yards from the crest.

Battalion and regimental command posts, as well as artillery observation points, are located on the crest of the second row of hills, to make possible observation of both German and Soviet positions.

It is the opinion of the German High Command that reverse slope positions have many advantages over positions built on forward slopes. The attacking side has difficulty in organizing ground reconnaissance and in delivering direct artillery fire on such positions. Furthermore, the commander of the attacking forces finds it hard to direct operations, especially after his forces have gone over the crest and entered combat on the reverse slope.

TACTICS IN TRENCH WARFARE

In their endeavor to make use of the advantages, and to reduce the disadvantages, of trench warfare, the Germans have been giving particular attention to defensive tactics and to the organization of counterattacks.

The break-through of their forward line is viewed by the Germans as the most critical moment for defensive action. They therefore make every effort to reestablish the former position as quickly as possible. According to instructions issued to the 270th Grenadier Regiment, units occupying the trenches must immediately launch a counterattack, even with small forces. It is pointed out that the slightest delay will enable the opponent to consolidate his gain and develop it in depth. The initial counterattack is conducted by personnel in first-line trenches.

The Germans counterattack simultaneously in a number of directions (not less than two). The self-propelled guns or tanks, awaiting the signal for counterattack, are usually concealed in a forest—at the crossing of lanes within or at the edge of the forest. Where there is no forest, the tanks or guns stand concealed behind a hill.

In this connection it is interesting to note new employment of self-propelled guns, such as the Ferdinand. The Germans have been using these guns to fire from fixed positions. To protect them from Soviet fire, the Germans prepare tank trenches which the guns occupy as soon as the counterattack starts. These trenches afford protection against artillery fire, since only the gun barrel is exposed; the mount is masked by an earth breastwork. Not always, however, is this protective device employed. In open terrain the Ferdinands merely come out of their hiding places and open fire. When they cease firing, they back into their hiding places and thus avoid open maneuver on the battlefield.

To reduce vulnerability of trench defenses after a penetration has taken place, the Germans endeavor to convert communication trenches into switch positions running at right angles to the front line. Instructions to the 270th Grenadier Regiment included the following comments:

"When the enemy succeeds in driving a wedge into our defenses and occupies a section of the trenches, he immediately tries to spread over that section and attack our firing points with the aid of deeply echeloned shock groups. In this case the enemy will gain an advantage in relation to our machine-gun points, automatic arms, and rifles. Under these conditions trenches offer no opportunity for deployment, since anyone trying to come out will be shot down. This danger is greater when the trenches are not continuous. Furthermore, a trench protects the attacker from his own fire, either flat or high trajectory."

SHIFT TO JUNCTURE

When a trench system is endangered by an enemy penetration, the Germans rapidly shift all soldiers in the first line trench to the juncture of the communication trench and the main trench. Here they deploy and make themselves ready to meet the attack. Earth barricades are erected in the main trench close to the communication trench, and from them fire is directed on the abandoned positions to prevent new enemy troops front entering. If the Germans are able to prevent penetration into the second and third line of trenches, and succeed in arresting the Soviet advance on the flanks, they then endeavor to regain the first trench. With this in view they employ the communication trench as a switch position and from it launch a flanking counterattack.

Prior to the arrival of company and battalion reserves, the counterattack is usually conducted by the infantry units posted in the front line. These forces are divided into two groups: A storm group consisting of the unit leader and two soldiers armed with automatic weapons and hand grenades; and a group of grenade throwers consisting of four soldiers, of whom three are armed with hand grenades and one with a rifle-grenade thrower. At a given command the grenades are thrown into the first bend of the trench. Following the explosion, the storms group rushes forward, firing its automatic weapons. This group is followed by the grenade throwers. The team occupies the trench bend and makes preparations for repeating the maneuver to take the next section of the trench. If successful in capturing a large portion of the first trench, the Germans then endeavor to extend their defensive action to prevent further penetration of the Soviets into the second and third line of the defenses.

In these operations local counterattacks are conducted by company reserves posted in the second line of trenches and battalion reserves brought up from the rear. The principal blow during these counterattacks is delivered by way of communications trenches leading to the front line. This is done with the purpose of driving wedges into time enemy's formations occupying the captured positions. If the counterattack is successful in disrupting the line of troops occupying the first trench, the subsequent clean-up is accomplished by the methods described above.

While engaged in trench combat, the German infantry offers no opposition to the opponent's tanks, letting them pass to the rear defenses where they are met by the cannon and antitank guns sited in depth. At the same time artillery, mortars, and heavy infantry weapons direct their fire beyond the first trench line to prevent the enemy infantry from reaching the trench.

THE FALSE FIRST LINE

A German attempt at new methods of surprise and deception is revealed by use of a false first line of defense in trench warfare. At one time, while waiting for the termination of Soviet artillery preparation, the Germans took cover behind earthworks or moved to the second or third line of trenches. With the shift of the Soviet artillery fire to the depth of their position, the

Germans rapidly moved back to the first line of trenches and met the attacking infantry with concentrated fire. This procedure, however, lost its effectiveness as soon as the Soviet soldiers and officers discovered the ruse. Orders were then given to Soviet artillery to shell the front line of German trenches a second time, following the firing in depth.

The Germans then adopted new tactics. They left the first line of trenches unmanned by infantry, posting there only a number of observers with flares and a few roving machine-gunners. In this way they hoped to deceive the Soviet observers by giving the impression that a large number of firing positions were to be found in the most advanced trenches. The Soviets then discovered that their artillery preparation directed toward the first trench line failed of its purpose, as the main German forces were located at the second or third line of trenches. Frequently the Soviet infantry would attack and occupy the first system of trenches, to discover that this was only a trap. (In some instances the bottom of the trench was mined.)

With these tactical measures, the Germans used new methods of counterattack. In a recent order to the German troops the following instructions were given: "The main line of defense should be occupied by as small a number of infantry as possible: reserves will be located in the rear and used for relieving front-line units and delivering counter blows. . . . In this way losses can be avoided from excessive massing of troops at the front line during an expected attack by the enemy."

Accordingly, the battle formation in a sector defended by a battalion was as follows: One company distributed in small groups along the second line of trenches; the other two companies kept farther in the rear, reserved primarily for counterattack and acting, as a rule, in small mobile groups (one or two platoons). Each group had from two to five tanks or self-propelled guns attached.

SOVIET OFFENSIVE TACTICS

In trench warfare Soviet officers emphasize the importance of reconnaissance, aggressive attacks rapidly followed through, and concentration of fire on vital points. Their views are summarized herewith:

The account of the structure of German defenses makes clear how important it is for the attacking side to maintain adequate reconnaissance. The attacker must know in advance the structure of the enemy's defenses and discover its vulnerable points. Among such points are the firing positions of artillery and heavy infantry support weapons, the areas of tactical reserve concentrations, the command posts, and the main communication centers leading from the centers of resistance and switch positions to the trenches.

Attacking troops must take into account the enemy's tactics, to meet his tricks with their own devices. Before infantry goes into action, artillery must concentrate its blows on the areas where the enemy's most important firing positions are located. Artillery and mortar fire, and infantry and tank attacks, must be so directed as to paralyze the defense, disrupt it into isolated parts, and effect a break-through in the entire depth.

Of particular importance is the fight against German artillery observers located in first-line trenches. To eliminate enemy observation points must be the task of artillery, infantry, and particularly of snipers.

Combat experience has demonstrated that best results are attained by attacking trench sectors where communications trenches connect with the first trench line. In such cases Soviet troops, after capturing the first trench, spread through the communication trenches to the second and third line, disrupting the entire defense system and destroying its defenders in hand-to-hand combat.

Rapid and decisive action is essential to success. The enemy must be prevented from retreating and erecting a defense at the junction of communication trenches and the first trench line. These areas should be attacked immediately by infantry using large quantities of hand grenades. While fighting is going on in the first trench line, artillery and mortars direct their fire upon the second trench, aiming particularly at the intersection points of the communication and main trenches in order to disrupt reserve formations and prevent a counterattack.

In attacking enemy positions, infantry should never stop at the first line of trenches but should break through to the enemy's main positions. Experience has shown that it is important to assign small groups to exterminate German machine gunners stationed at the first line of trenches—ordinarily in flanking positions and at angles of trenches—as well as to protect against possible ambushes. (Ambushing has been practiced by the Germans on a large scale.)

In the break-through of reverse-slope defenses it is especially important to determine the character of the forward edge and to eliminate the enemy's firing points in that edge. Observation points must be placed on the slope facing the enemy as soon as the attack begins. This will enable the attacking side to give effective artillery support to infantry units and tanks after they have entered the enemy's defenses in depth. It will also make possible effective direction of the attack. It has been found that the greatest success in overcoming German defenses was achieved by Red Army units which learned to attack violently without stopping at the forward edge. They break through in depth at once, leaving it to specially designated groups to handle such enemy resistance points which remain intact.

SOVIET TANKS IN CITY FIGHTING

Intelligence Bulletin, June 1946

Special Assault Units Used in Battle for Berlin

In the battle for Berlin, a large city converted by the Germans into a fortress for a last ditch stand, the Russians used massed mechanized units in street battles. However, Soviets do not recommend that tank units be sent into the city, where movement is usually restricted and channelized, barricades and obstacles easily prepared, and every building becomes a potential strongpoint and direct-fire gun emplacement, but the lessons learned during the battle of Berlin are worthy of attention.

Writing in "Red Star," an official Red Army publication, a Major N. Novskov details what was found in Berlin, the difficulties encountered, and some of the methods used to overcome the stubborn German defense.

For the battle of Berlin, the Russians organized combined assault detachments, consisting of one tank battalion, a rifle battalion, a company or platoon of engineers, a battalion of artillery (not less than 122-millimeter), and a platoon of flame throwers.

Fundamentally, the defense of Berlin was based on three defensive belts, with intermediate strongpoints: the outer ring of defense along the line of lakes and canals: the ring of defense in the outskirts and suburbs; and an inner ring in the city proper.

The Germans had expected the assault to be made from the East and had concentrated their defenses in that area. Soviet tank units, however, attacked from the south, cutting off the Berlin garrison from the southern German armies which were to have constituted its defense in that sector. The attack in the southern sector moved swiftly, with the Soviets by-passing the main centers of resistance and driving quickly through the outskirts and into the suburbs.

One big obstacle that had to be countered in this first phase was the crossing of the Teltow Canal, where the Germans had demolished all the bridges or had prepared them for demolition. After a thorough reconnaissance, a well organized and

"Berlin shall remain German!" — that's what the sign on the wall claims, but the crew of this Red Army 122-mm self-propelled gun had something else to say about it. It was with artillery of this type that the Red Army fought into Berlin.

A group of Soviet 152-mm self-propelled gun-howitzers halt on the side of an avenue during the fight for Berlin. The Red Army broke into the German capital by using detachments of tanks, assault guns, infantry, and support troops.

coordinated assault was made on the canal and a crossing effected.

In the suburbs, the tanks had a certain degree of maneuverability, due to the larger number of gardens, squares, parks, and athletic fields. They were able to by-pass and envelop separate centers of resistance, to attack some defense fortifications from the rear, and to complete enveloping movements in some cases. Once enveloped, the defense zones in this area quickly collapsed.

In the center of the city, the nature of the fighting was quite different from the fighting in the suburban area. Many-storied buildings in solid masses reduced the maneuverability of tank units. The only avenues of advance were along the streets from building to building. Maneuver was not entirely prohibited, however, for heavily barricaded streets and strongpoints could be enveloped by way of adjacent buildings.

During the battle for the center of the city, the tanks were used in a supporting role to reinforce the infantry and artillery. The infantry cleared the buildings of antitank gunners who were concealed in the basements or in the lower floors. After the buildings had been cleared, the tanks would advance.

It was in this battle for the center of the city that the combined assault detachments proved their worth. The combined detachment was able to attack with well protected flanks, and could maneuver within the limits of two or three buildings.

The general plan of operations of the assault detachments was as follows: If the detachment met with obstructions, it by-passed the obstruction, or the sappers would blow up the obstacle under the cover of tank and infantry fire. At the same time, the artillery placed fire on the buildings beyond the obstruction, thus blinding the enemy defense and providing additional cover under which the flame throwers set the buildings afire. After demolition of the obstruction, the tanks then rushed forward and tried to get past the enemy defense zone, while the infantry cleared the enemy from the zone itself. Flanks were protected along the side streets by self-propelled mounts or by tanks.

This basic plan was, of course, subject to variation. Depending upon a number of elements, such as the nature of the enemy fortifications, the enemy power of resistance, and the composition of the attacking elements, the tank battalion can attack along two or three streets. Major Novskov asserts that it is better to attack along three streets, keeping the reserve in the center. When the attack is successful along any of the streets, the attacking force is then able to maneuver and envelope the stronger portion of the defensive zone. A tank attack along a larger number of streets leads to a dispersal of force and a reduction in the rate of attack.

Each tank brigade ordinarily had as a main objective the envelopment of from four to six buildings. In the accomplishment of its mission it was found to be of special importance to have a mobile reserve capable of commitment in the direction of the main effort.

Major Novskov states that the boldness of the tankmen played a great role in the street battles. When artificial obstructions were not present, the tanks, with motorized infantry dismounting at high speed, dashed through certain buildings to intersections, squares, or parks, where they took up positions and waited for the infantry. When the infantry had cleared the enemy from the buildings that had been passed by the tanks, the tanks again moved forward in the same manner. When a defended obstacle was encountered, the tank first tried to by-pass it. When it proved to be impossible to by-pass the obstacle, and only when it was impossible, they would begin assault operations.

An example of the action of one assault group is cited by Major Novskov. "While attacking in the direction of the Ringbahn (loop railroad), the tank battalion was stopped in the northern part of Mecklenburgische Strasse by a reinforced concrete wall 8 meters wide and 2.5 meters high. The barricade was protected by strong machine gun and automatic fire and also by antitank grenade launchers installed in houses at the barricade itself. There were no detours. The commander decided to break through the obstacle. He first sent out a group of submachine gunners whose mission was to annihilate the grenade launchers, which was accomplished in a short period of time. Then 122-millimeter guns opened fire on the houses where the enemy firing points were located. The tanks, advancing simultaneously with the artillery, also opened fire on the buildings on the other side of the barricade. Under cover of the artillery and tank fire assault engineers climbed up to the barricade with explosives. After three explosions in the barricade, a breach was made through which tanks and infantry rushed. The well organized mutual support guaranteed the success of the attack."

In the case of Berlin, used as an example of a large modern city turned into a fortress, the Russians emphasize the importance of mobile reserves; the formation of cooperating

Red Army T-34 tanks rendezvous in the rubble of a Berlin square. During combat in the city, Soviet tank battalions, supported by infantry, assault guns, and engineers, attacked on an average front of two to three city streets wide.

teams of tanks, infantry, artillery, and engineers; the importance of heavy artillery ("not less than 122-millimeter"); and the fact that maneuver though restricted by the channelized avenues of advance, can still be performed on a limited scale.

The Soviets further note that the use of massed tanks in the streets of a modern city is not recommended, but that it has been done, and tanks can be used effectively if it is done correctly.

They emphasize the importance of not dispersing the attacking force too greatly, and of attacking on a relatively narrow front for each assault detachment.

More from the same series

Most books from the 'Eastern Front from Primary Sources' series are edited and endorsed by Emmy Award winning film maker and military historian Bob Carruthers, producer of Discovery Channel's Line of Fire and Weapons of War and BBC's Both Sides of the Line. Long experience and strong editorial control gives the military history enthusiast the ability to buy with confidence.

The series advisor is David McWhinnie, producer of the acclaimed Battlefield series for Discovery Channel. David and Bob have co-produced books and films with a wide variety of the UK's leading historians including Professor John Erickson and Dr David Chandler. Where possible the books draw on rare primary sources to give the military enthusiast new insights into a fascinating subject.

Barbarossa

Eastern Front: Encirclement

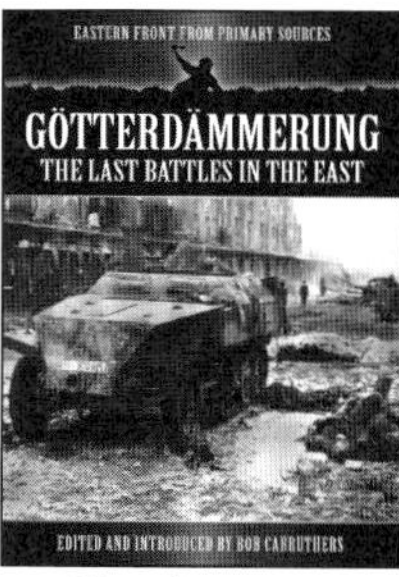

Götterdämmerung

Eastern Front: Night Combat

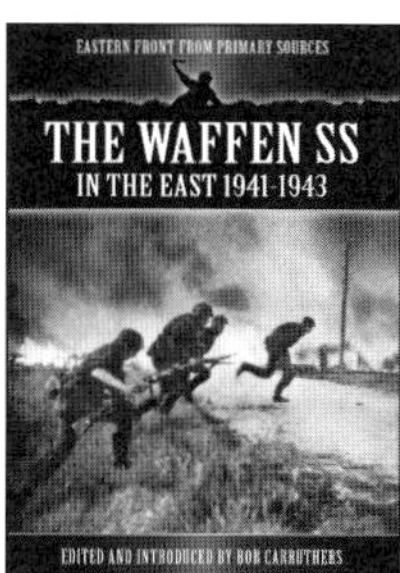

The Waffen SS in the East 1941-1943

The Waffen SS in the East 1943-1945

The Wehrmacht Experience in Russia

Winter Warfare

The Red Army in Combat

Wehrmacht Combat Reports: The Russian Front

For more information visit www.pen-and-sword.co.uk